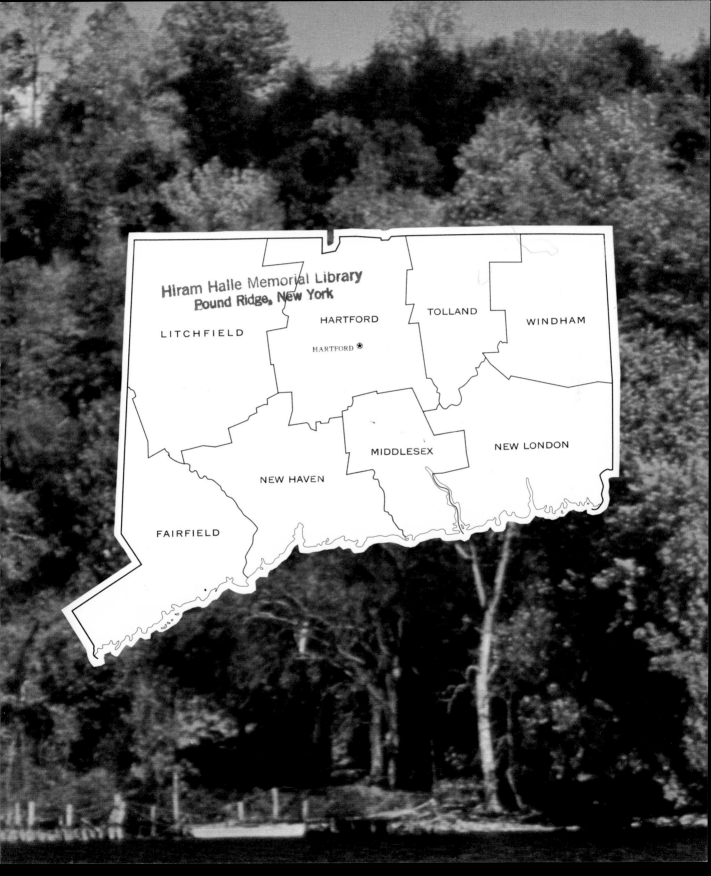

LITCHFIELD

HARTFORD

HARTFORD ✪

TOLLAND

WINDHAM

NEW HAVEN

MIDDLESEX

NEW LONDON

FAIRFIELD

The New

Enchantment of America

CONNECTICUT

By Allan Carpenter

 CHILDRENS PRESS, CHICAGO

ACKNOWLEDGMENTS

For assistance in the preparation of the revised edition, the author thanks:
BARNET D. LASCHEVER, Director of Tourism, Department of Commerce, State of Connecticut, and ANTHONY DAVENPORT, Department of Commerce, State of Connecticut.

American Airlines—Anne Vitaliano, Director of Public Relations; *Capitol Historical Society*, Washington, D. C.; *Newberry Library*, Chicago, Dr. Lawrence Towner, Director; *Northwestern University Library*, Evanston, Illinois; *United Airlines*—John P. Grember, Manager of Special Promotions; Joseph P. Hopkins, Manager, News Bureau; Carl Provorse, *Carpenter Publishing House.*

UNITED STATES GOVERNMENT AGENCIES: *Department of Agriculture*—Robert Hailstock, Jr., Photography Division, Office of Communication; Donald C. Schuhart, Information Division, Soil Conservation Service. *Army*—Doran Topolosky, Public Affairs Office, Chief of Engineers, Corps of Engineers. *Department of Interior*—Louis Churchville, Director of Communications; EROS Space Program—Phillis Wiepking, Community Affairs; Charles Withington, Geologist; Mrs. Ruth Herbert, Information Specialist; Bureau of Reclamation; National Park Service—Fred Bell and the individual sites; Fish and Wildlife Service—Bob Hines, Public Affairs Office. *Library of Congress*—Dr. Alan Fern, Director of the Department of Research; Sara Wallace, Director of Publications; Dr. Walter W. Ristow, Chief, Geography and Map Division; Herbert Sandborn, Exhibits Officer. *National Archives*—Dr. James B. Rhoads, Archivist of the United States; Albert Meisel, Assistant Archivist for Educational Programs; David Eggenberger, Publications Director; Bill Leary, Still Picture Reference; James Moore, Audio-Visual Archives. *United States Postal Service*—Herb Harris, Stamps Division.

For assistance in the preparation of the first edition, the author thanks:
John N. Dempsey, Governor; Ella Grasso, Secretary of State; Norman E. Delisle, Connecticut Education Association; Joseph R. Swan, Development Commission, State of Connecticut; Connecticut State Chamber of Commerce; Bridgeport Area Chamber of Commerce; and Greater New Haven Chamber of Commerce.

Illustrations on the preceding pages:
Cover photograph: Mystic Seaport, Connecticut Development Commission
Page 1: Commemorative stamps of historic interest
Pages 2-3: Gillette Castle, Connecticut Development Commission
Page 3: (Map) USDI Geological Survey
Pages 4-5: Hartford area, EROS Space Photo, USDI Geological Survey, EROS Data Center

Project Editor Revised Edition
Joan Downing
Assistant Editor, Revised Edition
Mary Reidy
Library of Congress Cataloging in Publication Data
Carpenter, John Allan, 1917-
Connecticut.
(His The new enchantment of America)
SUMMARY: Discusses the history, natural resources, and famous citizens of the Constitution State and describes numerous places of interest.
1. Connecticut—Juvenile literature.
[1. Connecticut] I. Title.
II. Series.
F94.3.C3 1980   974.6   79-4173
ISBN 0-516-04107-X

Contents

A.M. Williard captured the "Spirit of '76" in his famous painting. Perhaps they were playing "Yankee Doodle."

A True Story to Set the Scene

"YANKEE DOODLE WENT TO TOWN"

There was a great commotion in the hen yard. Down flew about. Dust swirled, and there was much indignant cackling as the hens lost many of their best feathers. An excited colonial lady hurried out to the road in front of her house waving handfuls of bright plumage at a group of horsemen waiting impatiently there. "Soldiers should wear plumes," she cried, and made each man put a feather in his hat.

The lady was Elizabeth Fitch of Norwalk, and the horsemen were a shabbily dressed force commanded by her brother, Colonel Thomas Fitch, governor of Connecticut from 1754 to 1766. They were just starting from Norwalk for service in the French and Indian War. When Miss Fitch came out to bid them good-bye, she was horrified that they had no uniforms and looked so little like soldiers. With her hastily gathered feathers she tried to improve them.

When Colonel Fitch and his men arrived for duty at Fort Cralo, near Renssalaer, New York, they were still wearing the feathers, which made them the subject of much joking, some of it good-natured and some not. "Now stab my vitals," British army surgeon Dr. Shuckburgh, is supposed to have said, "they're macaronis!" Macaroni was the slang word used at the time to describe a dandy or overdressed person.

Dr. Shuckburgh was so amused by the appearance of Colonel Fitch's troops that he later sat down and wrote a poem about them in which he used the now-famous phrase "and called it macaroni." The poem, eventually set to music, how or by whom no one is quite sure, became "Yankee Doodle Dandy," Connecticut's state song.

Dr. Shuckburgh thought he was being sarcastic. But the colonists everywhere loved this jibe at their supposed backwardness. "Yankee Doodle" became one of the inspirations of the Revolutionary War and has been a well-loved part of our folklore ever since—all this from a Connecticut chicken yard.

Perhaps the story is typical of the Yankee ingenuity of Connecticut, which has always been able to provide a lot from very little.

The Hadlyme ferry crosses the Connecticut River.

Lay of the Land

RIVERS OF QUINNEHTUKGUT

The Indian word *Quinnehtukgut* means "by the long tidal river" or "upon the long river." If the word is pronounced with its initial "Q" like a "K" it is easy to see how the modern spelling and pronunciation of Connecticut came about.

Of course, that "long tidal river" is the Connecticut River, which divides the state almost into equal halves. The Connecticut and Housatonic rivers are the only ones in Connecticut on the United States geological survey list of principal rivers of the country. The Housatonic and its tributary the Naugatuck River drain the western highland country of Connecticut. Navigation on the Housatonic extends to Derby. The Connecticut River is navigable as far as Hartford, and the tides are felt to about the same point.

Another important Connecticut river is the Thames. Its "drowned valley" forms one of the deepest harbors on the entire Atlantic Coast. The Thames river system with its tributaries the Quinebaug, Yantic, and Shetucket drains the eastern area of the state.

Other Connecticut rivers include the Mad, Pequonnock, Salmon, Weekeepeemee, Pootatuck, Whitfords, and Pomperaug. The gorge of the Mianus River is one of the most primitive spots within a short distance of metropolitan areas on the coast.

The state's largest body of fresh water—Candlewood Lake—is formed in an unusual manner. During hours when electricity is not being used at peak, hydroelectric power created by the river's current is used to pump water from the Housatonic River into the basin of the lake, and in this way the lake itself is kept filled. As the water cascades back down from the lake, it creates more power.

Other Connecticut lakes include Terramuggus, Waramaug (called "one of the most beautiful natural bodies of water in the state,") Gaillard, Saltonstall, Compounce, Wamgumbaug, Hammonasset, Quassapaug, and Barkhamsted Reservoir. One of the most interesting bodies of water is the tiny, deep-green lake right on the top of the Green Pond Mountain.

STORY OF THE LAND

Many times Connecticut was covered by ancient seas. Upheavals of the earth formed mountains, sometimes pushing deposits of those early seas high into the air. Through the ages these mountains were worn down by erosion. At least three times volcanoes poured lava over the countryside. Once more the earth moved and tilted to form new mountains, and these in turn were worn down until much of the region again was plains. Slow-moving mantles of the Ice Age covered much of Connecticut, probably reaching into Long Island Sound. Most of the lakes and waterfalls of today were created by action of the glaciers.

In many parts of the state the various periods and geological times have been exposed to view. The formation of the earth over a period of 325,000,000 years is visible in a section known as the "Great Unconformity," near Southington.

Today, in general, the land of Connecticut is an old plain, gently tilted, with the land rising gradually from Long Island Sound to an average elevation of about 1,000 feet (304.8 meters). The state occupies about half of what is called the New England Peneplain. The central valley of the Connecticut River and the coastal plain are relatively flat. In other parts, forested hills and intimate valleys follow one another in quick succession. The highlands to the north and west are the ends of the Green Mountains and the Berkshires, which reach their greatest heights farther north.

The village of Moodus in East Haddam has long been plagued with "supernatural" noises. Terrifying rumbles as if giant boulders were rolling down a slope, screeches, eerie groans, and explosions like artillery fire come from the earth. The Indians said the noises were the work of spirits, and some of the settlers blamed witches. Cotton Mather called it the "voice of an angry God."

Today scientists know that Moodus occupies an unusual position where many "fault" lines come together. As the earth settles slightly along these lines, it makes groaning noises. When it settles more sharply, of course, earthquakes occur, as in 1791 when chimneys toppled and cracks opened in the ground.

12

Rural Kent is typical of the state's rolling beauty.

CLIMATE

New England has a reputation for rugged climate, but Connecticut is comparatively mild. There are only about ten days each year when the temperature goes above 90 degrees Fahrenheit (32.2 degrees Celsius) and only three, on the average, when it falls to 0 degrees Fahrenheit (-17.8 degrees Celsius) or below. The growing season is fairly long, with the first killing frost about mid-October and the last in mid-April. In spite of the state's small size, there is some variety in climate. Temperatures in the higher altitudes of the northeastern and northwestern sections are lower in both winter and summer than those in the central valley or along the shore.

13

*Remains of the original inhabitants are
preserved at Tantaquidgeon Museum, Uncasville.*

Footsteps on the Land

LAND OF THE SACHEMS

Not much of unusual interest has been discovered about the people who lived in Connecticut before historic times, although there are many favorite locations where prehistoric relics are found. One of these is Sackett's Cave near Killingworth.

In the period before and just after Europeans came to the region, Connecticut was the scene of some of the bloodiest wars on the continent. The Pequot Indians were among the most cunning and ferocious Indians in New England. The Pequot and Mohegan Indians, related to the Mohican, formed one Indian people who have been classed as one of the four main Indian groups in Connecticut. The others were Sequin or "River" Indians, the Matabesec or Wappinger Confederacy, and the Nipmuck.

The Nipmuck lived in the northeastern corner of the region; the Pequot-Mohegan territory centered around Groton; the River Indians were a group living in the central area under the rule of one *sachem*. Indian rulers in the region often were known as sachems or "sub chiefs," rather than chiefs. In present-day western Connecticut, the Matabesec were compelled to share their hunting grounds with the Mohican of eastern New York.

Among the local clan names of the Matabesec were the Uncowa, Wepawaug, Siwanoa, and Pootatuck; River Indians included Poquonnuc, Tunxis, Wangunk, Podunk, Machimoodus, Quinnipiac, and Hommonasset. All of the Indian groups of Connecticut were dominated by the powerful Mohawk group, who frequently invaded Connecticut territory in order to keep the groups there under their control.

One of the most important and most interesting illustrations of Indian life in Connecticut was the palace of Chief Waramaug of the Pootatuck.

This palace, near New Milford, was a "long house" probably 100 feet (30.5 meters) in length and 20 feet (6 meters) wide, covered with bark carried for many miles on the backs of laborers. The main council room was decorated with brightly colored portraits of the leader, his family, and counselors. Other rooms were brightened with colorful animal pictures. The best Indian artists, borrowed from other groups, came from great distances to complete this unique work of primitive art.

Following the Indian custom after Chief Waramaug's death, each Indian who passed by his grave heaped a stone on it, as the Indians generally did in tribute to a dead leader. Ironically, the main house of the Hurd estate was built over this particular grave.

Fish and sea food were important to Indians in the region. Shell heaps such as the one covering 24 acres (9.7 hectares) near Milford have remained to show how much the Indians depended on sea food. Once a group of Nipmuck Indians invited the Narragansetts from Rhode Island to a feast of eels. When the visitors complained that the food had been cooked without dressing, the Nipmucks promptly killed all but two of their guests in the fight that followed.

There were probably about 5,000 Indians in present-day Connecticut when the first Europeans arrived there, although some less reliable estimates place the figures at a much higher number. Today almost no Indians are left in the state. The vigorous and primitive place names of Indian origin are the principal reminder throughout Connecticut of the people who once called the land theirs.

GETTING A FOOTHOLD

In 1614, Dutch explorer Adriaen Block discovered a great river (the Connecticut) and sailed upriver as far as Enfield Rapids, trading with the Indians. In 1631, Wahquinnacut, sachem of the Podunk Indians, journeyed to the young Massachusetts towns of Plymouth (in its eleventh year) and Boston (in its second year) to invite Europeans to settle in the valley of the broad river of Connecticut. He hoped this would strengthen his people in the continual struggle with their ancient enemies, the Mohawk and Narragansett.

The next year the governor of Plymouth, Edward Winslow, visited the Connecticut Valley to see the quality of the lands, and a group of Englishmen under Lord Say secured a grant from the Earl of Warwick to all land west from Narragansett River (now the bay) "to the south sea," the Pacific Ocean. The alarmed governor of nearby New Netherland purchased land from the Indians at the mouth of the Connecticut River and had his men nail up the Dutch coat of arms on a tree at a point the English called Saybrook.

Less than a year later, the Dutch established a fort and a trading post on land bought from the Pequot Indians on the site of what now is the city of Hartford. In that same year William Holmes, representing the English Plymouth Colony, erected a fortified trading post where Windsor later grew. As Holmes sailed by the Dutch fort, the commander called out, "Strike your colors or we will fire." But Holmes replied, "I have the commission of the governor of Plymouth to go up the river and I shall go." When the Dutch later sent a force to drive out the intruders, they found the English so well fortified they gave up the effort. In the first winter, seventy of the Windsor people had to return to Plymouth because of the severe weather, and those who stayed behind suffered greatly and barely kept the trading post going.

In 1634, John Oldham led a large party from the Massachusetts settlement of Watertown to a spot he had discovered the year before, south of the Dutch trading post. This became the community of Wethersfield. Since this was the first community in Connecticut founded as a settlement rather than a trading post, Wethersfield claims distinction as the oldest permanent settlement in the state.

In October 1635, fifty people under John Steel from Cambridge, Massachusetts, came to settle what was first called Suckiagu. This was very close to the Dutch fort, and later came to be called Hartford. Saybrook was also established at the mouth of the Connecticut River in 1635, but it did not flourish and was abandoned in 1644.

So, clustered rather close together, surrounded by wilderness, were the three little communities that became the first towns of Connecticut. Actually, this might be called the first western movement and settlement, which later was to carry clear across the continent.

If those pioneers had not been made of sturdy stuff, the English

The Museum of the City of New York exhibits a model of Adriaen Block's ship the Onrust, *meaning "restless."*

community might not have endured. Although many of them went back to their former homes, some stayed on. Then in 1636 "a reinforcement of more than one hundred persons led by their pastor, the Reverend Thomas Hooker, brought new life to the dying colony. Wisely, they made their journey down from the Bay in the spring of the year, hewing a road before them through the wilderness, singing the ancient Psalms of David as they drove their herds along it. So they came to the great river, and from their coming the three little towns of Wethersfield, Windsor and Hartford grew and flourished by the riverside."

Fear of the Indians was the main problem of the colony. After frequent attacks, the General Court of Hartford drafted ninety men from Hartford, Windsor, and Wethersfield under Captain John Mason. With reinforcements from Saybrook and some friendly Indians, they advanced on the main Indian palisade at Pequot Hill, West Mystic. Taking the fort by surprise, Mason's army burned the Indian encampment. Six or seven hundred Pequot were burned; about seven were captured and seven escaped. This has been called "the most decisive battle ever fought on Connecticut soil."

Cotton Mather described the scene: "The greatness and the violence of the fire, the flashing and roaring of the arms, the shrieks and yells of men and women and children within the fort and the shouting of Indians without, just at the dawning of the morning, exhibited a grand and awful scene. It was a fearful sight to see them frying in the fire and the streams of blood quenching the same."

After the remnants of the Indian army were defeated in a swamp near Fairfield, a treaty of friendship was made between the English and the Indians, and Captain Mason became the first military hero of Connecticut.

A NEW HAVEN FOR PURITANS

In 1638 the Reverend John Davenport, a Puritan minister from London, and a merchant from his congregation, Theophilus Eaton, led about two-hundred-fifty pioneers from Boston to the shores of Long Island Sound and founded New Haven. They purchased a large area of land from the Indians for twenty-three coats, twelve spoons, twenty-four knives, twelve hatchets, and miscellaneous scissors and hoes.

At first the people of New Haven signed a covenant agreement to be governed by the laws of Moses. Then, after a year, a civil government was set up with the "Word of God" as the absolute rule. "Seven Pillars" of the church were elected as the leaders, and Theophilus Eaton was chosen first governor of the Colony of New Haven. Only members of the church were allowed to vote, and the colony became what is known as a Puritan theocracy.

The colony was extremely strict. Its "blue laws" provided the death penalty to any son who cursed or struck his parents. Elder Malbone publicly flogged his daughter Martha on the New Haven Green because she had a date with a young gentleman of her acquaintance. Quakers were branded, whipped, and banished from the colony.

A CHARTER TO CHERISH

Meanwhile, in January of 1639, the three original towns to the north had grouped together into what they called "One publike State or Commonwealth." Inspired by Thomas Hooker's sermons, in which he outlined the principles of a just government, Roger Ludlow drew up a document for governing this new organization. This document, called the Fundamental Orders, has been praised as the first practical constitution to declare that "the foundation of authority is in the free consent of the people." They formed a model for much of the U.S. Constitution. John Haynes was elected first governor of the new Connecticut colony.

The Dutch trading post and fort were surrounded by the English settlement. Cut off from almost all the Indian trade, it was finally abandoned. In 1654 the English colony took over the fort without a shot, in the name of the king.

John Winthrop, Jr., was elected governor of the Connecticut colony in 1657 and again in 1659. Because the legal rights of the colony to its land were in considerable doubt, Winthrop sailed to England to see what he could do. The results of his negotiations were amazing, although exactly how he accomplished them has never been explained. In 1662 the king granted a charter that legalized almost everything the colony had done, including its Fundamental Orders. In addition, the Connecticut colony was permitted to extend from the Massachusetts border to Long Island Sound and from the Narragansett Bay to the Pacific. It is interesting to note that if the boundaries had remained that way, the present cities of Cleveland, Ohio; Chicago, Illinois; Des Moines, Iowa; Omaha, Nebraska; Odgen, Utah; and Crescent City, California would all be in Connecticut.

This Connecticut charter was probably the most liberal ever issued by a British king. Connecticut was provided with more freedom than any of the other colonies and in many ways was almost independent. Wethersfield held a public election in defiance of the royal courts, and when fined five pounds, the town successfully refused to pay. This was probably the first demonstration of the American spirit of independence against the mother country.

By 1687, however, King James II decided to unite all the New England colonies under one government. Sir Edmund Andros was appointed governor. He at once demanded that Connecticut give up its precious charter. When this was not done, Andros went to Hartford with an armed escort. He conferred with local officials for hours and demanded that the charter be brought forth and surrendered. Finally this was done. Then suddenly the candles were put out, and

The Buckingham House kitchen in Mystic Seaport.

when they were again lighted, the charter had disappeared.

Tradition says that Joseph Wadsworth had slipped out with the charter and hid it in a hollow of an oak tree on Samuel Wyllys' property. From that time on the famous tree has been known as the Charter Oak, and the words "Charter Oak" have become one of the best-known phrases in Connecticut's history.

The harsh Andros government survived only two years, and Connecticut was able to go back to a government under its old charter.

A UNITED AND A GROWING COLONY

The boundaries of the Connecticut charter included New Haven as part of Connecticut. The government of New Haven objected strenuously to this. New Haven leaders felt the government under the charter was too free and easy. They even took up arms with the intention of defending their freedom. However, the Duke of York controlled the colony to the west, and it became apparent to New Haven that if it did not join with the Connecticut colony, it probably would be forced into the New York colony, which it felt was even more godless.

So after long negotiations, New Haven finally was united with the Connecticut colony in 1664. For 174 years, from 1701 to 1875, Connecticut had joint capitals, Hartford and New Haven, and alternate sessions of the legislature were held in each.

Almost forty years of peace with the Indians in Connecticut had followed the defeat of the Pequot. However, the fate in store for them became clear to the Indian leaders. They realized that soon the colonists would take over the entire region, and the traditional hunting grounds of the Indians would be lost.

Chief Philip of the Wampanoags in Rhode Island planned to unite the Indians of the northeast and drive the settlers away. He gathered strong forces, and for a time it appeared he might be successful. In 1675 the forces of Connecticut, including three-hundred colonists and three-hundred-fifty friendly Indian troops, joined with those of Massachusetts and Rhode Island in a desperate attempt to save themselves and their colonies. After a period of bloody massacres and battles known as King Philip's War, peace was restored, and Indian power in Connecticut was broken forever. Connecticut suffered considerably less than some other New England colonies.

In the more than one hundred years from the uniting of the Connecticut colony until the Revolution, the colony grew and took on a distinctive character of its own, while remaining almost independent. The colony was one of the most self-sufficient in the New World. It produced most of what it needed and it required comparatively little trade with the outside world.

History "lives" in the nineteenth-century Mystic Seaport village.

However, by the 1760s Connecticut men were moving freely about the globe. Men from Granby took part in the British attack on Havana, Cuba, in 1762, and by 1763 there was a growing trade between Connecticut ports and the ports of the West Indies, Newfoundland, and the Atlantic ports of the other colonies.

Boundary disputes with Pennsylvania, Rhode Island, Massachusetts, and New York were settled—peaceably for the most part.

Litchfield Congregational Church

Yesterday and Today

CONNECTICUT IN THE REVOLUTION

Because of Connecticut's traditional independence of the mother country, it is not surprising that the colony took an early part in protesting the increasing interference of Britain in the affairs of the colonies. As early as 1770, the freemen of Lebanon met and drafted a declaration of rights and liberties—an interesting document six years ahead of the Declaration of Independence.

In protest against the hated British tax on tea, Old Lyme had its own little "tea party." The people of the town took tea from the sacks of a traveling peddler and burned it on the village green.

When war finally came, Connecticut was better prepared than some of the other colonies. Preparations for war had been under way for more than a year. The town of Wethersfield was the only community that was able to send militiamen to Cambridge in uniform to take part in those first critical battles of the Revolution.

Even the colonial governor, Jonathan Trumbull, took the side of the colonists. He was the only royal governor of all the colonies to renounce his loyalty to the king and continue in office after the Revolution began.

Because it was Governor Trumbull's home town, Lebanon became an early center of Revolutionary activity. Its war office served as a kind of northern headquarters. For the Revolution, Connecticut is said to have "furnished more men and money than any other colony except Massachusetts." Connecticut soldiers served in the forefront of the battle line from Quebec to the Carolinas. Nor should the service of the Indians in the Revolution be forgotten. As an example, the Schaghticoke Indians alone provided a hundred warriors for the Continental army.

No call for aid to Connecticut ever lacked response during the entire war. To help alleviate the suffering at Valley Forge, the citizens of Hartford collected thirty thousand dollars, and Moses Goodman delivered it to the ragged troops in 1777. When Washington's forces again were starving in 1780, the general, hardly daring to hope for more help, sent word of his desperate situation to Governor Trumbull. Almost as quickly as the word came, off trundled a train of oxsleds, burdened with three thousand barrels of pork and fifteen hundred barrels of beef. As Washington wrote in his diary, "No other man than Trumbull would have procured them and no other state could have furnished them." In fact, Washington nicknamed Connecticut "The Provision State."

Factory and forge in Connecticut also turned out the necessities of war. Wartime planners conceived the idea of stretching a huge chain of iron across the mighty Hudson River at West Point to keep British ships from sailing up that vital waterway. The anvils at the forges of Lime Rock rang with the clash of steel as the great 3-foot (.9-meter) links were shaped. The amazing chain was completed and carted overland to the river. Some of these links may still be seen at the Chicago Historical Society Museum.

The forges of Lime Rock also produced the guns for the undefeated warship *Constitution*. The first American warship, named the *Oliver Cromwell,* was built in the shipyard at Essex.

While no great and decisive battles of the Revolution were fought in the state, a large number of Connecticut communities suffered attacks during the war, especially coastal cities and towns. Important skirmishes were those at Stonington, attacked from the sea in 1775, Danbury in 1777, New Haven 1779, and Bridgeport and New London in 1781.

In the attack on Danbury, the town was burned and looted, but property of Tories, those who sympathized with the British, was marked and saved. Black Rock Fort at the entrance to New Haven Harbor resisted the British. One of the tragedies of the Revolution occurred at Groton. Under the direction of the traitor, Benedict Arnold, watching across the river, the defenders of Fort Griswold were slaughtered. Lieutenant Colonel William Ledyard had quickly gathered one-hundred-fifty militiamen to defend the fort just before the British stormed it. They brutally killed Colonel Ledyard and most of his brave men after they had surrendered. Eighty-five militiamen died, but their brave fight left one-hundred-ninety-three British dead. After the fort fell, the town was looted and burned, and

Governor Jonathan Trumbull was one of the most important figures of the American Revolution. Trumbull's portrait is by Harry Ives Thompson.

many men of the town were killed. In the Avery family alone, nine men were killed and three wounded.

Many brave men of Connecticut, noted and unknown, played key roles in the Revolution. The "one-man victory" of William Tully is famous in Connecticut lore. Tully, alone, was in charge of contraband goods seized in the war, when a British force of eight men tried to take the goods. Tully aimed his flintlock and dropped two men with one shot. The others fled, terrified. Tully received credit for a victory in which the enemy received "25 percent casualties" without any casualties on the American side.

Another lone patriot "attacked" a British force as they marched through the Bethel Parish of Danbury. This local man fired on the advance guard and shouted orders to an imagined American army in the woodland. This daring patriot almost succeeded in stampeding the British single-handedly.

Two hundred men of Guilford under Lieutenant Colonel Meigs

dragged their whaleboats overland at Plum Gut, Long Island. Launching them on the ocean side, the troops set fire to one hundred tons (91 metric tons) of hay, burned ten transport boats at wharves, set fire to an armed schooner, and returned unharmed in twenty-four hours. When the British in turn attacked Guilford, the men of the town put up such a spirited fight the enemy retired after burning only two houses.

More American privateers, private vessels licensed as warships, sailed from New London than from any other port in New England. New London ships captured three hundred prize ships. The town was burned and blockaded by the British in an effort to cut down such heavy losses.

One of the most successful American naval officers in the Revolution was Captain Dudley Saltonstall of New London. He was the first American to unfurl the national flag on the high seas. Captain Saltonstall performed the remarkable feat of capturing New Providence at Nassau in the British Bahamas.

The town of Mystic was known to the British during the Revolution as "that cursed little hornet's nest."

The first chartered copper mine in America was designated an official Continental Army prison by George Washington. He felt that the mine shafts of New-Gate Prison at East Granby would hold prisoners securely. It became notorious and later was the state's first prison, until a new one was built above ground. It is now a major tourist attraction.

During the Revolution the newly established award of the Purple Heart, created by George Washington, was given to only three soldiers. It was Connecticut's unusual distinction that all three of the men who received this decoration were from the state. Sergeants Daniel Bissell, William Brown, and Elijah Churchill, "three of the most daring soldiers in the Continental Army," received the Purple Heart from George Washington personally.

Names of more famous Connecticut men in the Revolution included General Israel Putnam, Ethan Allen, and those two dissimilar figures who shared such unlike and unlikely fates—the tragic traitor Benedict Arnold and the tragic martyr Nathan Hale.

FIFTH OF THIRTEEN

After the war, changes came to Connecticut more slowly than to most of the other former colonies. When the Articles of Confederation proved unsatisfactory, one of the main problems in creating a new constitution was the claims of some seacoast states to lands in the west. Connecticut had never given up her nominal claim to land extending clear to the Pacific. At last, however, Connecticut agreed to relinquish all right to govern those lands, except her ownership rights to 3,250,000 acres (1,315,230 hectares) in northern Ohio, which came to be called the "Western Reserve." This included the region where the city of Cleveland is today, founded by Moses Cleaveland of Canterbury.

With this problem out of the way, Connecticut ratified the new Constitution of the United States, and on January 9, 1788, became the fifth state of the Union.

When that new national government received its first real test in the War of 1812, Connecticut was not in favor of the war. Her shipping and commerce had been hurt greatly by restrictions put on it before the war. The state's displeasure was shown by the fact that it refused to provide its militia for use by the federal government during the war.

However, Connecticut individuals and communities played prominent parts in the war effort. As it was during the Revolution, Stonington was again attacked from the sea. A British battle fleet, mounting a total of one-hundred-forty cannon, sent a fierce barrage of gunfire shoreward. Although the Connecticut militia had only two cannon, the local forces withstood this attack and only three of their men were wounded. The British lost ninety-four, and the British ship *Despatch* was almost put out of commission. Since that time, a favorite Stonington chant has been, "It cost the King ten thousand pounds to have a dash at Stonington." The many British cannon balls later found in the nearby woods have become among the most valued relics of the community.

When Commodore Stephen Decatur and his tiny fleet took shelter in New London harbor, pursued by the British navy, most of the townspeople fled. When a messenger from the fort was sent to collect old rags for gun wadding, Anna Warner Bailey (known as Mother Bailey) promptly took off her red flannel petticoat and declared, "There are plenty more where that came from." The men of the fort flew the red undergarment from their flagstaff as a symbol of courage and patriotism to inspire others in the region.

One of the most prominent Connecticut figures in the war was Commodore Thomas MacDonough of Middletown, who was the victor in the Battle of Lake Champlain, September, 1814.

CHANGES

Throughout all the colonial and early statehood days—a period of one-hundred-fifty-six years—the original Connecticut charter, with few changes, continued to serve the state. Connecticut was the only one of the Puritan commonwealths that remained under virtual domination by a state church—the Congregational.

By 1818, however, the state was ready for a change, and a new liberal constitution was adopted in that year. This basic law was drafted so well that it served the state until 1965, although often revised. In this Constitution, the right to vote was extended to more men, and the state rejected any "established" church. The power of a small "ruling class" was reduced.

Over the years, many thousands of Connecticut people left the state as pioneers to less settled areas. Northern New England, Pennsylvania, and New York distributed much of the land in its Western Reserve in Ohio to those who had suffered damages during the Revolutionary War and to veterans of that war, and many of these went to Ohio to take up their lands. By 1819, according to one estimate, 700,000 people had left the state and only 300,000 remained. It is probable that there are more descendants of Connecticut people in the Middle West than there are remaining in Connecticut.

Meanwhile, new thoughts and ideas were beginning to take hold in a way that would soon transform life in the state. The first tax-supported public library in the United States was begun at Salisbury.

Canals, turnpikes, and railroads encouraged movement of goods and people about the state. Two New London men were captains of the *Savannah,* the first steamship to cross the Atlantic under power. Captain Stevens Rogers was a sailing expert who would have taken over the ship if the power had failed, and his brother-in-law, Moses Rogers, was the steam captain.

Universal manhood suffrage, the privilege of voting for all men, was accomplished in Connecticut in 1845.

FROM THEN TILL NOW

As the dispute over slavery grew in violence throughout the country, Hartford became a center of antislavery sentiment. Many "stations" were set up on the Underground Railroad, designed to help slaves escape to freedom in Canada. One of the many noted stations was Hendee House near Andover.

When the Civil War came and President Lincoln called for men, fifty-four companies of Connecticut recruits volunteered—five times the state's quota. It was said that more of the men of Prospect fought in the war than there were registered voters in the town. Under the leadership of Civil War Governor William A. Buckingham, Connecticut remained ardent in its support of the Union cause. Unlike many early Civil War troops, the First Connecticut Regiment was so well equipped that General Winfield Scott exclaimed, "Thank God we have one regiment ready to take the field."

Altogether, the total number of men from Connecticut serving in the Federal forces was 57,379. Of Connecticut troops in the war, 20,573 were killed, wounded, missing, or died of disease as a result of the war.

The first Union general to die in the war was General Nathaniel Lyon, born near Chaplin. Leader of Federal troops in Missouri, he died helping to keep that state on the Northern side. It may probably be said that General Lyon was the man most responsible for holding Missouri for the North.

Another Connecticut man who died in the war, in a strange and

31

Connecticut is a leading state in the manufacturing of submarines. The first atomic submarine, the Nautilus, *was built at Groton.*

tragic way, was Captain S.L. Gray of Liberty Hill. Captain Gray was killed when his whaling ship was shelled off the remote island of Guam by the Confederate raiding ship *Shenandoah.*

Much of the modern history of Connecticut after the Civil War is concerned with growth and development of industry, agriculture, commerce, and transportation and communication.

However, a few interesting or important events and dates might be mentioned here. Connecticut's progressive spirit was illustrated again in 1911 when America's first code of law for registering airplanes and licensing pilots was established in the state. During World War I there was an unprecedented period of industrial expansion in Connecticut. There were 65,728 Connecticut men in the armed services during this conflict.

An unusual happening occurred in 1920 when Russian Count Ilya Tolstoi founded Churaevka, a village for "White" Russian refugees, mostly from the imperial army.

The great depression of the 1930s was especially severe in Connecticut. However, advances were made by the passage of many new laws and changes in the state constitution. During World War II, due to war contracts, employment and production in Connecticut reached new peaks. Connecticut led all states in production on a per-person basis. The number of men and women from the state in the armed services totaled 210,891; of these, 5,724 died.

Although it fortunately has never been used in war, one of the mightiest weapons of war came into being in 1954 when the *Nautilus,* the world's first atomic-powered submarine, was launched from the shipyards at Groton. Later, such submarines were made even more awesome when the Polaris type was developed at Groton. This kind of nuclear sub has the capacity to deliver atomic weapons from underwater.

In 1958, for the first time in eighty-two years, Democrats gained control of the Connecticut General Assembly and most of the state offices. In that same year the scenic Connecticut Turnpike was opened.

Connecticut took a step in 1960 that was unique in American government. County governments were abolished and all functions of county government were transferred to the state government. Consequently, Connecticut is one of the few states having no county organization. Local government is carried out through an extension of the township system. Many of these "towns" contain several villages with different names. Each village may have its own churches, stores, post office, and railroad station, but these villages do not have any government of their own. They merely share in the government of the whole "town." For example, the villages of Salisbury, Lakeville, Lime Rock, and Taconic all have their own names and post offices, but are all part of the town Salisbury.

The popular governor of Connecticut, Abraham Ribicoff, resigned in 1961 to become the nation's Secretary of Health, Education and Welfare. Later, he was elected to the U.S. Senate. In 1965 a new constitution was adopted. In 1975 Ella T. Grasso took office as the first woman governor to be elected "on her own merit." That is, she was the first woman governor who had not been previously connected to the office by a husband who was governor.

THE PEOPLE

Of Connecticut's population, over a million were born in some country other than the United States. Another 700,000 are natives of Connecticut who have one or both parents of foreign birth. More than 40 percent of the people in the state are of foreign birth.

The largest ethnic groups now in Connecticut are Italian, Canadian, Polish, English, Irish, Scottish, Welsh, German, Russian, and Puerto Rican. There are nearly 200,000 blacks, and of the original owners of the state—the Indians—fewer than a thousand remain in Connecticut. In religion, Catholics are now a majority.

The inventive, shrewd, careful people of the state early gained the nickname of "Connecticut Yankees." The Connecticut Yankees of today may be of different backgrounds, but according to Connecticut leaders, "The people of Connecticut are aggressively aware of their future. . . . Throughout the state, there is the unmistakable hum of dynamic activity—planning for the future, building and rebuilding, analyzing the advantages and seeking new business and industry to enjoy them, forecasting and trying to provide for the needs of the people—employment, health and safety, recreation, education and, in general, the means for the good life. Today's Connecticut Yankee insists upon it as his heritage."

34

Natural Treasures

Those who think of Connecticut as almost solidly populated and as a continuous succession of cities and towns may be surprised to know that almost two-thirds of the state is still in woodland. There are twenty-eight state forests and seventy-nine state parks in Connecticut. The tradition of conservation of such valuable natural resources is an old one in the state. Many early Connecticut people, such as the Shakers, were pioneer conservationists. Shaker Elder Omar Pease was the first person ever to plant a forest in America.

The People's State Forest, between Pleasant Valley and Riverton, is probably unique in the country. This forest land was purchased for state preservation with money donated by thousands of individuals. Cathedral Pines, near Cornwall, is one of the finest stands of towering, virgin white pine in the East.

Native dogwood ornaments the countryside, with its snowy blossoms in the spring and with its spectacularly colored autumn foliage. Maples and other colorful trees, against a background of the evergreens, add their display to the fall scenery for which New England is justly famous.

Beautiful pink and white blossoms of the state flower, the mountain laurel, splash the countryside in springtime, as does the azalea. Among the most attractive of the hundreds of wild flowers scattered over field and forest are the delicate orchids, pyrola, Indian pipe, and the gaudy cardinal flower.

For the most part, only small animals such as skunk, woodchuck, red and grey fox, and muskrat are found in Connecticut, although some white-tailed deer and a few mink and otter also flip gracefully through the more hidden reaches of the state.

Connecticut is on the edge of the eastern "flyway" where migrant birds of great variety stop on their way north or south, depending on the season. Native birds include the orchard oriole, fish crow, clapper rail, warblers, Louisiana water thrush, seaside sparrow, brown creeper, junco, northern water thrush, white-throated sparrow, and such game birds as ducks and ruffed grouse.

One of the earliest important writings on conservation of bird and animal life was inspired in Connecticut. The poet Henry Wadsworth Longfellow was visiting near Killingworth. When he observed the common custom of farmers shooting birds as pests, he wrote *The Birds of Killingworth* as a protest against such slaughter.

Right: Some deer can still be found. Below: A blue jay.

People Use Their Treasures

THE "CONNECTICUT YANKEE"

Much of the soil of Connecticut was stony or unproductive, so the people of the state were forced at an early date to look for other means of making a living. Necessity required them to use their wits to create, from what little they had, things that other people needed and would pay for. The ingenuity that they developed in this became famous far and wide, and the name Connecticut Yankee soon came to mean the same as "clever fellow."

They dammed and harnessed the streams for power to turn out an amazing variety of products. Since there were comparatively few raw materials in the state, the products they turned out made special use of the skills and abilities of the people. The inexhaustible fund of Yankee ingenuity is illustrated by the fact that in proportion to population more patents have been issued to Connecticut inventors than to those of any other state.

The first American patent ever issued to a woman went to Mary Kies of South Killingly for a machine to weave silk and straw.

The list of Connecticut "firsts" in business and commerce is amazing.

The whole system of modern manufacture using interchangeable parts originated in Connecticut with Eli Terry and Eli Whitney. Separately they worked out the details of a new system in which each part made for any manufactured item was almost identical to another. This meant that they could be assembled without costly and time-consuming fitting and adjusting. It also meant that if any part wore out or broke, it could be replaced easily. Whitney introduced these production methods in his firearms plant at Hamden.

The first, standardized, interchangeable clock movements were produced by Eli Terry at Plymouth (Todd Hollow) in 1802. Terry's invention of the shelf clock in 1814 brought clock prices from twenty-five dollars to five dollars. Chauncey Jerome was another pioneer in the use of interchangeable metal parts in clockmaking, and his efforts led to founding of the famous New Haven Clock

*Connecticut's clock making
traditions are kept alive at Mystic Seaport.*

Company. Bristol was an early and continuing leader in clock manufacturing with the Ingraham and Sessions companies. A former partner of Terry, Seth Thomas established the great clock firm bearing his name and the town where the factory was located was named Thomaston in his honor.

The first ax factory in the world was set up at Collinsville by David and Samuel Collins and their cousin, William Wells. Before this time, axes had to be specially ordered from blacksmiths. Two blacksmiths, Barnes and Rugg, produced the first machine-made bolts in America, eliminating tedious hand-threading processes.

Phineas and Abel Pratt built the first machine for cutting the teeth of combs, and they sold their first combs in 1799. The Pratt family may hold the record for the length of time in which an American business has been owned continuously by the same family.

The first copper coins made in the colonies were struck at Simsbury as early as 1737. In 1744 John Higley produced the first ton of American-made steel, at Simsbury. Nails had been made in Connecticut and exported before the year 1716. The first tinware in the United States was made at Berlin in 1740.

Colonel David Humphreys operated the first successful large-scale woolen mill in the United States at Seymour in 1806, although the first woolen mill in New England had been set up at Hartford eighteen years earlier. The first cotton thread manufactured in the United States was produced at Willimantic.

The first American hat factory was started at Wethersfield in 1750, and the first beaver hat factory was established at Bridgeport by Zado Benedict, producing three hats per day.

Cigars were first made in America at South Windsor. Packaged garden seeds were introduced at the Enfield Shaker Colony in 1802. The first "knockdown" furniture was produced by famous chair designer Bert H. Hitchcock of Riverton, who shipped his chairs in parts ready for assembly by the buyer.

In 1812 Connecticut introduced the use of steam power for manufacturing at the Middletown Woolen Manufacturing Company. New Haven had another distinctive first in the world's first commercial telephone exchange. The first American plows were produced at Wethersfield, and a machine for sawing ivory was invented by John B. Collins at Hartford. The first American carpet mill was established at Thompsonville in 1828, and the first hoop skirts were made at Derby. America's first drawn-brass pipe and wire were produced by Israel Holmes of Waterbury in 1831. Thomas I. Howe of Derby invented and used the first machine that made pins in one operation. Coe Town (now Beacon Falls) had the first American friction matches in production. Israel Coe made the first spun-brass kettles in America at Wolcottville (Torrington). Derby produced America's first tacks, and Waterbury the first hook-and-eye fasteners.

Other interesting and important Connecticut "firsts" include American shaving soap, silver-plated spoons, cylinder lock, spool-wound silk thread, derby hat, condensed milk, bicycle factory, standard accurate measuring machine, trading stamps, mechanical player piano, football tackling dummy (devised by Amos Alonzo Stagg at Yale University in 1899), and successful gun silencer.

Few factors have had a greater influence in American business and industry than trade associations. There now are thousands of these in almost every field. This great and significant movement was started in 1853 with America's first trade association, the American Brass Association, started by Naugatuck Valley manufacturers.

Pioneering in the field of metal working has been one of Connecticut's great contributions. Among numerous Connecticut accomplishments in this field, the great anchor for the *Constitution (Old Ironsides)* was forged at Mt. Riga and drawn to the Hudson River by six yoke of oxen. The guns for another famous ship, the *Constellation,* were cast in the Ethan Allen Forge at Lakeville.

The state leads in some metal work. It produces more ball bearings, aircraft engines, and firearms than any other state.

Connecticut has long held a dominant place in the manufacture of firearms. Both in war and peace, well over half of all the small-arms ammunition comes from Connecticut plants. The Winchester, Colt, Marlin, and Remington companies of Bridgeport are world famous. Similar leadership in the silver field is held by Insilco of Meriden and Wallace Silversmiths of Wallingford.

Waterbury is considered the brass capital of the United States. One of the world's leaders in educational toys is the A.C. Gilbert Company of New Haven, creator of the Erector set and pioneer in model-train manufacture. Hartford is noted for one of the outstanding makers of pipe organs—the Austin Organ Company.

Another industrial pioneer was the Pratt and Whitney firm. They were the first to make measuring devices of great precision, and also led in engine manufacture. Connecticut retains the leadership it gained long ago in the field of hat manufacturing, and East Hampton is still known as the "bell town" because of the production of all kinds of bells—from sleigh bells and hand bells to large carillons.

MARKETING PIONEER: THE "YANKEE PEDLAR"

Almost as soon as Connecticut manufacturers began their businesses, they faced the problem of where to sell their wares. With the use of modern manufacturing methods, of course, they produced far more than could be sold in the immediate neighborhood. Some of the more adventurous manufacturers set out on foot with packs on their backs.

In 1740, the Pattison brothers, William and Edward, created the first tinware made in America; what they made first they sold by calling on their neighbors. As they manufactured more tin goods, they hired any number of adventurous, traveling salesmen. Ultimately, some of these covered routes as long as 1,500 miles (2,414 kilometers). As time went on the number of peddlers, generally known as "pedlars," increased. They added buttons, pins, needles, combs, clocks from Eli Terry's factory, and later added a glittering array of hard-to-get products to their line. When they approached a house, whole families turned out—and in the remote areas, entire communities. In the beginning Uncle Sam's reputation for salesmanship was mostly earned through the sales skill of the Yankee pedlars, who brought to isolated people not only goods from the outside world but the news and some of the "glamour" of faraway places as well.

As one sales traveler wrote in the 1840s, "In Kentucky, Indiana, Illinois, Missouri and here in every dell in Arkansas and in every cabin where there is not a chair to sit on, there was sure to be a Connecticut clock." The Yankee pedlars invented their own version of the installment payment plan. Many of them reached to far corners of the earth. As an example of this, most of the buildings at Parimaribo, capital of Surinam, were put up by Connecticut traders.

"INSURE IN-SURE INSURANCE"

Connecticut may be called the "Insurance State" and Hartford the "Insurance City." The insurance business began in Connecticut

A "Yankee pedlar"

when Hartford was a seaport, and ships sailed down the Connecticut River to begin their profitable voyages to the West Indies and other areas. There were great risks on those voyages. The shipowners got together to find a way to share the risks. A plan was worked out. Each owner paid a certain amount into a common fund. If something happened and he suffered a loss, he would receive a certain amount from the fund.

The first formally organized insurance companies began when the Hartford Fire Insurance Company issued its first policy in 1794, and the first insurance company was incorporated in the state in 1795. This was the Mutual Assurance Company of the City of Norwich. The first insurance firms were fire insurance companies, followed by life, accident, and casualty insurance firms.

In 1835, New York City had the greatest fire ever experienced until that time in the United States. It wiped out the Wall Street business section, causing twenty million dollars worth of damage. One of the Hartford insurance companies with losses to pay was owned by Eliphalet Terry. After traveling by sleigh through the winter snows to New York, he is said to have jumped on a soapbox near the smoldering wreckage of seven hundred buildings and announced to all of his policyholders that they would get their money. Although Terry's company's share of the $20,000,000 loss was only $64,974, the dramatic way in which he demonstrated Hartford's reliability immediately brought a rush of business.

Hartford fire insurance companies weathered the great Chicago fire as well as those in Jacksonville, Boston, and Baltimore. In the great San Francisco earthquake and fire, Hartford companies met a total of $15,000,000 in claims.

In 1864 the Travelers company issued the first American accident insurance policy. As the country grew and became more complex, need for other kinds of insurance multiplied. The first American automobile insurance was written at Hartford in 1898, and such specialized insurance as that for steam boilers originated there.

Today there are forty-five insurance firms in the "insurance state," employing more than thirty-five thousand people. There are nearly one hundred million policies with Connecticut companies, and the benefits paid yearly are several billion dollars.

FARMING UNDER A BLANKET

From the air, large sections of the Connecticut River Valley appear to be huddling under cotton blankets. For nearly four hundred years tobacco has been grown on a small area of about 61 square miles (about 158 square kilometers) in this region. Today, that area grows some of the world's best tobacco. Broadleaf and Havana tobacco leaves were the earliest types grown in Connecticut. They were used as the outer "wrapping" of cigars. When tobacco grown in Sumatra became popular for wrappers, Connecticut tobacco seemed to be losing out.

Secretary of Agriculture James "Tama Jim" Wilson imported some Sumatra tobacco. He later wrote in his annual report, "...After preliminary experiments in the summer of 1899, some Sumatra tobacco was planted under shade in the spring of 1900 (in Poquonock). The leaf produced has been so fine that the New York tobacco men say that it cannot be told from the imported Sumatra leaf. They predict, as a result of this work, a complete revolution of the tobacco business in the Connecticut Valley."

His words were prophetic. The secret is in two words used in Secretary Wilson's report—under shade. By covering the Connecticut fields with cotton cloth, growers gave the plants an even temperature, the high humidity, and the same protection that Sumatra plants received from the island's low-lying heavy clouds.

Today, more than half a century after the experiments, Tobacco Valley produces over two-thirds of all wrapper tobacco used by American cigar manufacturers. Only a small part of this comes from sections of the valley not in Connecticut.

To make the tents used for "shade," 5,000 yards (4,572 meters) of cloth, 50 cedar poles, and 350 pounds (158.8 kilograms) of wire are required for each acre. The cloth has to be replaced each year because it becomes frail after a summer in the sun.

Before shade-grown tobacco can be marketed, seed must be planted in seed beds. Then the ground and tents are prepared, seedlings replanted and cultivated, disease controlled, buds broken off to develop the leaves, and sucker shoots eliminated. The leaves are picked by hand. They are then sewn together in pairs, then placed on laths in curing sheds, where they change from green to brown under carefully controlled conditions of heat and humidity.

Tobacco leaves are taken down in just the right conditions of

Tobacco is grown under a blanket and the leaves are picked by hand.

humidity to keep the leaves from breaking. They are tied into "hands," and then are "fermented" in the warehouse. Next comes grading according to color, texture, and quality of the leaf. The leaves are baled in a special baling process and each bale is wrapped in woven grass mats imported from Borneo or special paper mats made in this country. The bales are carefully marked according to grade and size of leaf. Then, "the world's finest shade-grown tobacco" is shipped to markets around the globe.

The skill and care necessary to produce the Connecticut tobacco crop illustrates the investment and know-how needed in almost every type of production in the modern world.

In the latest agricultural census, there were only slightly more than four thousand farms in Connecticut, but these had the highest average value per acre of any state in the union. The total annual value of farm products in Connecticut is more than $250 million. Dairy products make up more than a third of this—poultry and poultry products more than a fourth, with field crops only about a sixth.

"DOWN TO THE SEA IN SHIPS"

Much of Connecticut's maritime glory is in the past, but it is a glorious past!

The first great commercial shipping venture of Connecticut took place as early as 1647. The traders of New Haven built the *Great Shippe* and filled it with their finest produce and products. When it was ready to sail to England, the *Great Shippe* had to be towed stern first through ice to open water. This was a sign of bad luck to superstitious sailors. More bad luck was forecast when the Reverend Mr. Davenport intoned, "Lord if it be Thy pleasure to bury these, our friends, in the bottom of the sea, take them; they are Thine; save them."

No news was ever heard of the *Great Shippe* or her crew again. However, there is a legend that she came back to New Haven as a ghost ship, sailing into port full-rigged against the wind and finally plunging beneath the surface.

Shipbuilding began at Derby on the Housatonic River in 1657, and shipbuilding at New London dates from 1664. The first American ship to enter the trade with the West Indies was the *Tryall* of Wethersfield. The first Connecticut ships for the China tea trade were built at Middle Haddam, and there the noted shipbuilder Thomas Child launched 237 vessels.

As the period of the clipper ship drew to a close, Connecticut took the lead in building the new ships. The modified clipper ship *Andrew Jackson,* built in Mystic by Irons and Grinnell, broke the New York to San Francisco sailing record of the *Flying Cloud* by nine hours. The merchant ships *Dakota* and *Minnesota,* built in 1900 at Groton, were the largest of their day, displacing 33,000 tons (29,937 metric tons) each. The Groton shipbuilding industry continues today, turning out the most advanced ships ever created—nuclear submarines.

Because of their skill in shipbuilding and seamanship, Connecticut sailors early turned to the two most daring and profitable activities of the sea at the time—whaling and sealing. Stonington was known as "the nursery of seal men" and had a large fleet of whaling vessels. It was also important in other shipping activities as well as in shipbuilding. New London's whaling fleet numbered only one ship less than the world's leader—New Bedford, Massachusetts.

Connecticut whalers roamed the seas of the world seeking the great, elusive, ocean-going mammals. The first steam whaleboat afloat, the *Pioneer,* was built in New London and brought back a cargo worth $151 thousand on her first voyage.

Sealing ships from New Haven and other Connecticut ports roamed the cold waters of Patagonia and other faraway seas to bring back the valuable pelts of those fur-bearing animals. In a good year one hundred thousand sealskin pelts might be unloaded at Stonington alone.

Steamers to New York and other ports plied Long Island Sound and the navigable rivers of Connecticut for many years. Some fishing fleets are still at work, but oysters are now "farmed" in such waters as those off Milford. This practice has been growing ever since it was found that oysters could be "planted, cultivated, grown, and harvested," much as crops on land.

46

The Charles W. Morgan *preserves the whaling tradition.*

MINERALS AND FORESTS

Although lumbering once was important, the forests of Connecticut today do not provide very much timber for cutting. At one time, however, primitive sawmills were active throughout the state. Millington Green is a ghost town reminder of the old lumbering days. The Butters Sawmill has been operating since 1688, and is the oldest in the country.

In 1793 an attempt was made to grow mulberry trees in Connecticut. The state sent a half ounce (about 14 grams) of mulberry seed to every town in Connecticut, and the legislature placed a bounty on the trees. The state had been caught up in the boom for growing silkworms, which eat only mulberry leaves. For a while it appeared that the drive would be successful. Mansfield was producing more silk by 1830 than any other town in the United States. However, a blight in 1845 destroyed most of the mulberry trees, and the local industry turned to imported silk. However, silk is still important in Connecticut manufacturing.

While Connecticut is not one of the great mineral producing states, mining operations in the state produce about fifty million dollars worth of products every year, and the value has been steadily rising. The most important minerals today are sand and gravel, stone, limestone, and feldspar.

Many minerals were more important in Connecticut's past and supplied the early industries with such vital materials as iron and copper. When iron ore was discovered at Salisbury in 1732, the strike brought a stampede to the town and a boom much like latter-day gold rushes in the West. The iron work contributed greatly to the Revolution.

The stone quarries of Portland provided much of the building material for the brownstone houses of New York City. In addition to building materials, Strickland Quarry near Portland has yielded beryl, garnet, quartz, and other minerals. Nearby Cobalt was the scene of mining operations for cobalt, which produced a deep blue paint. It is interesting to note, also, that Guilford granite was used in the foundation of the Statue of Liberty.

TRANSPORTATION AND COMMUNICATION

Cross-country travel in Connecticut developed slowly. Most people stayed at home in the early days or traveled as little as possible. However, the first post rider on the American continent traveled across the Connecticut countryside following the old Pequot Path from New York to Boston. Later the Boston Post Road became the established overland route from New York to Boston, crossing Connecticut by way of Hartford. It split into a number of alternate routes at various points along the way.

A Madam Knight made the tiresome trip in 1704 and reported,

48

"The Rodes all along this way are very bad, Incumbred with Rocks and mountainos passages, which were very disagreeable to my tired carcass . . . in going over a Bridge under which the River Run very swift, my horse stumbled, and very narrowly 'scaped falling over into the water; which streemly frightened me. But through God's Goodness I met with no harm." Later, in the Stamford region, she encountered ". . . many and great difficulties, as Bridges which were exceeding high and very tottering and of vast Length, steep and Rocky Hills and precipices. Buggbears to a fearful female traveler."

The Connecticut Turnpike, Merritt, and Wilbur Cross parkways are road-building masterpieces, designed particularly to retain the beauty of the rolling, colorful Connecticut countryside. Highways 84, 86, 91, and 95 are important parts of the transcontinental highway system.

With nearly 20,000 miles (32,187 kilometers) of roads outside of cities and towns, Connecticut ranks high in mileage of improved roads in proportion to the size of the state.

As did most of the other states at the time, Connecticut entered a vigorous canal building period. The Farmington Canal was chartered in 1822. This was part of a grand project that was designed eventually to connect Long Island Sound with the St. Lawrence River. The canal was opened from Cheshire to New Haven in 1828, but it lost money each year and finally suspended operations in 1847.

The Windsor Locks Canal, completed in 1829, was designed to carry river traffic around the rapids and also to furnish waterpower. This canal was operated until quite recent times.

The railroads did away with much of the value of canals. The first Connecticut railroad, the New York and Stonington Railroad, was chartered in 1832. Although railroad mileage has declined in recent years, Connecticut still has a large amount of trackage for its size. There are over 700 miles (1,127 kilometers) of railroad in the state today. The New York, New Haven and Hartford Railroad (now called the New Haven Railroad) has its headquarters in New Haven.

In the field of publishing, Connecticut has many "firsts." The Hartford *Courant,* founded in 1764, is the oldest daily newspaper in America with a continuous name and circulation. The first publica-

Old State Prison and copper mine, East Granby,
America's first chartered copper mine, 1707.

tion for young people in America also was founded at Hartford. This
was *The Children's Magazine,* first published in 1789. America's first
cookbook was also published in Hartford in 1796. The first foundry
for casting printing type was established at New Haven by Abel
Buell.

The first printing press in Connecticut began its work at New London in 1709, and the first volume printed in Connecticut was the
articles of organization of the Congregational Church. Connecticut
publishing over the years was particularly noted for its many
almanacs, including *The New England Almanac and Farmer's Friend.*
One of the most widely recognized scholarly publishing houses is the
Yale University Press.

Human Treasures

REVOLUTIONARY PATRIOTS

Of the many Connecticut people who served their country in extraordinary ways during the Revolutionary War, some of the names are among the best known in history. Others deserve greater recognition than they generally have received outside of the state.

One of these unsung heros is Israel Putnam, who also fought with distinction in the French and Indian War. When he returned from that war to his farmhouse near Brooklyn, many of his friends and acquaintances stopped to visit him. These visitors made such demands on his hospitality, his wife thought they should buy an inn; there he could suggest charging for his hospitality without seeming to be indelicate. They bought the Burdick Tavern at Brooklyn.

Local tradition says that Putnam was plowing a field here when he heard the news of Lexington and Concord. One of the famous stories of the war tells how he abandoned his plow in the field and without changing his clothes jumped on his horse and dashed to Cambridge. He arrived in time to become one of the commanding officers in the Battle of Bunker Hill. He also commanded troops on Long Island in 1776.

One of General Putnam's greatest contributions was holding together the troops of the American ''right wing'' under his command during the bitter winter of 1778-79. The camp where he quartered his troops at Bethel has been called the ''Valley Forge of Connecticut.'' General Putnam felt it was essential to keep a strong force at Bethal where they could march to the defense of West Point if needed or of the towns on Long Island Sound as required.

The ragged and poorly fed soldiers were ready to desert, and some of them already had formed a column to march to Hartford to ask for help. Only an impassioned speech by General Putnam, reminding them of their importance to the struggle for independence, kept the strategic force from breaking up.

General Putnam is noted for one of the most daring escapes of the Revolution. On February 26, 1779, the general was shaving in his

Putnam's
Daring Ride
*by Currier
and Ives.*

room at Greenwich prior to reviewing the Continental troops. When his mirror reflected a British force rapidly approaching, General Putnam ordered his outnumbered men to escape in whatever way possible. He himself jumped on his horse and galloped toward the brink of a cliff. The British were astonished to see his horse disappear over the edge and thought he had fallen to the bottom. However, with astonishing horsemanship, the general guided his horse from ledge to ledge down the wall of the cliff and escaped into the valley.

Another less well-known Connecticut figure of the Revolution was Governor Jonathan Trumbull, the only Colonial governor to take up the American cause. General Washington once said "except for Jonathan Trumbull, the war could not have been carried to a successful termination." In his "war office" Governor Trumbull held twelve hundred meetings of the Council of Safety of Connecticut. Plans of all kinds were made; troops were raised; conferences were held with leaders, including Washington, Adams, Jay, Benjamin Franklin, Lafayette, and Rochambeau. The governor's great ability in administration, organization, and the assembling of supplies was one of the major American resources of the Revolution. With a price placed on his head by the British, he often was forced to hide in his small secret room in order to continue his work.

Three members of the Trumbull family served as governors of Connecticut.

Another lesser-known Connecticut figure of Revolutionary times is Roger Sherman—the only man who signed all four of the fundamental documents of United States history. In addition, he helped to draft the Declaration of Independence as well as signing it.

The one patriot whose name has come to stand out above all others for sacrifice to his country is Nathan Hale, born at Coventry. He was teaching at New London when word came of the Battle of Lexington. Soon he shut up the school house on the hill and went to join Knowlton's Rangers. Of course, he never returned, and upon his execution by the British for spying he became probably the best-known American martyr. The words he is supposed to have said—"I regret that I have but one life to lose for my country"—are among the most familiar utterances of mankind.

Another well-known figure of the Revolution was Ethan Allen, born in Litchfield. This intrepid firebrand was authorized by the Connecticut General Assembly to recruit a regiment of Rangers to attack Fort Ticonderoga. On May 10, 1775, at the head of his men, Ethan Allen pushed through the gates of that fort. He arranged his troops in parade formation in the courtyard, got the British commanding officer out of bed, and while that officer was still in his night clothes Ethan Allen called for him to surrender the fort "in the name of the Continental Congress, by God!" Without a fight the British surrendered the strategic stronghold and also gave up valuable supplies.

Ethan Allen was known as an eccentric; among his beliefs was his conviction that after death man's soul entered any one of many kinds of animals, fish, snakes, or birds. He selected a large white horse to receive his soul after his death. In later life he published books making fun of the writings of Moses and the prophets, of the British army and the state of New York. Strangely, he died after a fall from a horse at Colchester.

53

INVENTIVE, ADVENTUROUS, SUCCESSFUL

Some of the most widely recognized inventors were natives of Connecticut or did their principal work in the state. Charles Goodyear, who invented the vulcanizing of rubber and made it possible for the nation to roll on wheels, was a native of New Haven. John Fitch, developer of a workable steamboat many years before Fulton, was born in East Hartford.

In 1848 the first cylinder lock in the world was created by Linus Yale at Stamford. Before that time, in 1833, Yale and his partner, Towne, had made the country's first revolving crane. The firm they founded, Yale and Towne, is well known.

Although he usually is better recognized as the inventor of the cotton gin, Eli Whitney's work of introducing quantity production methods in his firearms factory at Hamden was probably even more important to American progress. In 1855, Samuel Colt, inventor of the revolver, moved his Colt's Patent Fire Arms Manufacturing Company plant to Hartford. Here many of the present-day manufacturing methods were devised, and the plant served as a "training school" for several of the country's industrial leaders, including Francis A. Pratt and Amos Whitney, founders of Pratt and Whitney Company. One of the most ingenious developers of new manufacturing methods was Elisha K. Root, superintendent of the Colt plant.

Simon Ingersoll invented the friction clutch at Stamford; in 1858 he built and operated a steam wagon there—a forerunner of the automobile. Elias Howe, who perfected the sewing machine, was associated with New Hartford for many years.

At Hartford an entirely different kind of success was achieved by Horace Wells, who was the first to develop the application of anesthesia to dentistry.

Connecticut's eminence in clock manufacture included the work of such pioneers as Eli Terry of Terryville and Seth Thomas. Another clock pioneer was Benjamin Hanks of Litchfield, inventor of a tower clock wound by air; he became world famous for the casting of church bells in his foundry at Litchfield.

Eli Whitney Blake of New Haven was the inventor of a crusher for

54

stone. This brought the cost of road building down to the point where large-scale highway construction was possible. Milford was the home of Simon Lake, who invented the even-keel submarine. An earlier experimenter with submarines was David Bushnell, native of Westbrook. His submarine torpedo boat was tested successfully in several trials, but it failed to blow up any of the British fleet when tried in New York harbor during the Revolution.

A pioneer industrialist of Riverton was Lambert Hitchcock, whose work lives on today. In 1826 he began to produce the rush-seated, black or red chairs with their gilt stencil designs that have made his name famous. Originals of these chairs are eagerly sought as collector items, and duplicates are being turned out in many modern factories, including the original at Riverton.

Among early American industrialists, one of the most humane as well as successful was General David Humphreys.

General Humphreys was the first to import merino sheep (a superior breed) to this country. When his flocks prospered, he used their wool in the first large-scale woolen mill to be set up in the United States, which he established in 1806. He was the first man to build a complete model factory town for his workers, and one of the first industrialists anywhere to take an interest in the comfort, education, and welfare of his employees. He promoted legislation for state inspection of factory conditions. One of General Humphrey's most advanced ideas was the establishment of a self-contained village for orphans; he supported and outfitted them himself, and many became prominent in later life.

At an even earlier date, 1799, Simeon North was the first man to receive a contract for making government pistols at Berlin and might be called the "first" industrialist. Collis P. Huntington, who started his business career as a Yankee peddler, became a leading financier, supplying capital for such mammoth enterprises as the Southern Pacific Railroad.

Another financier of Connecticut, one of the most famous men of his day, was the legendary J. Pierpont Morgan, born in Hartford. Many of Morgan's ancestors, including his father, a merchant, were prominent in Hartford life.

One of Connecticut's greatest leaders in the insurance field was Colonel Jacob L. Greene. Moses Cleaveland, who founded Cleveland, Ohio, only to have the spelling of its name changed, was a native of Canterbury.

Among Connecticut adventurers and explorers was Nathaniel B. Palmer of Stonington, who was only twenty-one years old when he discovered the Antarctic Continent. One of the island groups nearby was named Palmerland in his honor. Groton's Captain Joseph Warren Holmes sailed eighty-three times around Cape Horn, a record for that difficult voyage. Another Groton man, John Ledyard, gained fame as an adventurer and traveler; among his other feats was walking 1,400 miles (2,250 kilometers) from Stockholm, Sweden, to St. Petersburg, Russia. Ledyard had sailed with Captain Cook on the voyage in which Hawaii was discovered, and into China, Siberia, and the Arctic. He died in Cairo, Egypt, at the age of thirty-seven while preparing an expedition for exploring Africa.

Professor Othniel C. Marsh of Yale University was an explorer of a different type. He was the first to discover dinosaur bones in the United States, and his most important work was tracing the evolution of the horse.

PUBLIC FIGURES

One of the most successful of all political leaders in Connecticut was one of the earliest—John Winthrop Jr., founder of New London, who served as governor for eighteen years, beginning in 1657. His most amazing success was obtaining the almost unbelievable Connecticut charter from the king of England. In an entirely different field, Winthrop was noted as the "Father of American Chemistry," and he worked diligently to develop the minerals of the region.

Another governor was Oliver Wolcott of Litchfield, who served in that post for ten years. He was the second Secretary of the Treasury of the United States and also the first president of the Bank of America. Another prominent governor of Connecticut was Samuel

Huntington, who signed the Declaration of Independence and was president of the Continental Congress for three years.

Oliver Ellsworth of Windsor was the third Chief Justice of the United States. Samuel Nicholas of New London received the first officer's commission granted by the United States Marine Corps. At the age of only fifteen Captain Samuel Smedley of Fairfield commanded a privateer during the Revolution and earned a distinguished name on the high seas. By the end of the war he had captured more prize ships than any other privateer or naval officer. One of the captured British captains, amazed at his captor's youth, exclaimed, "There is little hope of conquering an enemy whose very schoolboys are capable of valor equaling that of trained veterans of naval warfare."

MINISTERS TO SOUL AND SPIRIT

The first Indian minister of the gospel ordained in New England was Samson Occum, who received his training in Eleazer Wheelock's Indian School, forerunner of Dartmouth College. In 1766 he went to England to raise funds to train "ye native savages of North America." In this spectacularly successful mission, as a result of his fiery appeals for funds, he collected fifty thousand dollars for the work.

The Reverend Timothy Edwards, father of Jonathan Edwards, was the first minister in the Congregational Church of South Windsor, and he served that charge for sixty-three years. His son Jonathan was born in South Windsor.

The Reverend Samuel Seabury was the first Episcopal bishop in America—at New London. Timothy Dwight, president of Yale University, was so successful in converting people to his conservative Congregational religion that his students took to calling him "Pope Dwight."

A Tory minister, Reverend Licentiate Baxter, was imprisoned in Connecticut's notorious New-Gate Prison because of his sympathy for Britain during the Revolution. He preached such a fiery sermon to his fellow Tory prisoners deep in the dungeons that they were inspired to rush the guards at the head of the ladder and made one of the few recorded escapes from that awful prison.

One of the leading artists of the state was John Trumbull, son of Governor Jonathan Trumbull. An unusual claim to fame of John Trumbull is that he passed the entrance examinations for Yale University at the age of seven. George Henry Durrie has been called the "first and best artistic interpretor of the Connecticut scene." Noted sculptor Paul Wayland Bartlett, born in New Haven, first exhibited his works in a French salon at the age of fourteen. Bartlett's statue of Lafayette stands in the courtyard of the Louvre Museum in Paris.

Harriet Beecher Stowe was born at Litchfield, and her *Pogamuc People* describes her early childhood in Connecticut. Her brother, writer, lecturer, minister, Henry Ward Beecher, was also a Litchfield native. Other writers associated with Connecticut include James Fenimore Cooper, who was expelled from Yale in 1805, and Eugene O'Neill, the famous playwright, who also wrote a daily column for the New London *Telegraph*.

In Perilous Escape of Eliza and Child, *artist Harry T. Peters pictures Harriet Beecher Stowe's most famous scene.*

58

One of the most "redoubtable" literary men who ever lived was Noah Webster, born at West Hartford. His monumental work in compiling a dictionary makes him, even today, considered a supreme authority in his particular field of the English language.

Connecticut's best-known writer was an adopted son—Samuel Clemens—Mark Twain. Twain settled in his beloved house at Hartford and during his seventeen years of residence there wrote most of his books on which his greatest fame rests. One of his collaborators was Charles Dudley Warner.

Among the nation's earliest and most distinguished literary societies was a loosely organized club of brilliant men who called themselves the "Hartford Wits." They had considerable effect on the thought of America.

Connecticut's well-known people in the field of music include Reginald De Koven, of Middletown, composer of *Oh Promise Me;* composer of hymns and other well-loved songs, Fanny Crosby of Bridgeport; and noted Meriden opera star Rosa Ponselle. Actress Katharine Hepburn was born in Hartford. Renowned "modern" composer Charles Ives was a native of Danbury.

SUCH INTERSTING PEOPLE

One of the most colorful and picturesque Americans of all times was Phineas Taylor Barnum, born at Bethel in 1810. He began his career as a showman by exhibiting Joyce Heth, a black woman, who claimed to be the nurse of Geroge Washington and one hundred sixty years old. He gained great fame by exhibiting the dwarf Tom Thumb (Charles Stratton) who was just over 2 feet (.6 meter) tall. After a colorful wedding, Tom Thumb brought his tiny bride, Lavinia Bump Warren, to live in the Tom Thumb House in Bridgeport.

Barnum went on to spectacularly successful tours in Europe. He brought the European singer Jenny Lind to America, with a salary of one thousand dollars per night for one-hundred-fifty nights; then he went on to establish "The Greatest Show on Earth." In his circus, he

A portrait of Mark Twain, Samuel Langhorne Clemens.

established many methods of moving and handling men and materials that have been copied by military men everywhere.

However, Connnecticut remembers Barnum best as "Bridgeport's most beloved citizen."

He encouraged industries to establish plants in the city, helped Bridgeport get a harbor and worked for improved railroad service, water supply, and parks. He served as the city's mayor, and in 1936 Bridgeport issued a centennial "half dollar" carrying Barnum's likeness. In fact, some have said that except for the efforts of P.T. Barnum, "Bridgeport might be nothing but a wide place in the road."

Chief Uncas, Grand Sachem of the Mohegan group, holds a lasting place in the region's history. When Uncas was besieged by the Narragansett in Fort Shantok, near his headquarters, his food supply was exhausted and he and his men faced surrender and death. When Lieutenant Thomas Leffingwell of Saybrook heard of this, he loaded a canoe with supplies and managed to slip into the fort with enough food to save the day. From that time on, Uncas was one of the great Indian friends of the Europeans.

Among the early people of interest in Connecticut were Generals Edward Whalley and William Goffe. It was Whalley and Goffe who, as English judges, signed the death warrant for King Charles I. When the monarchy was restored they fled England and lived for four desperate years in hiding in Connecticut. Finally, when pressure against them eased, they moved to Massachusetts.

Elihu Burritt has been called "New Britain's most famous son." At the age of fifteen he started to learn the blacksmith's trade, studying Greek and Hebrew and other subjects whenever he had a moment away from the anvil. By the age of thirty, he was familiar with almost fifty languages and was known as the "Learned Blacksmith." He became one of the great promoters of world peace and was called "Apostle of Universal Brotherhood." Peace conferences were held in Paris, London, Brussels, and Frankfort because of his efforts. He returned to New Britain, where he died in 1870.

Another Connecticut man known for his compassion was Captain Stephen Snow of Milford, who nursed sixty-four Revolutionary war prisoners who had smallpox, until Snow himself died of the disease.

The strange career of Abel Buell included making the first map engraved in this country. Called "one of the most inventive geniuses of his time," for some unexplained reason he turned to counterfeiting. His punishment was "light." He had a small nick cut from his ear, but he was allowed to keep it warm on his tongue so that it could be replaced. And he had the letter "F" branded on his forehead, but placed so high it could be covered with hair. Buell invented the first lapidary machine in the country, for cutting stones, during his stay in prison, and his sentence was ended when he gave the king's attorney a handsome ring studded with gems.

Another strange career was that of Jemima Wilkinson of Ledyard. At her funeral she suddenly lifted herself from her coffin. She claimed that she had been raised from the dead as a redeemer and attracted a large following to her new sect—the Jemimakins. When they moved to New York, her followers pulled her to the new location in an elaborate chariot.

The extraordinary black, Venture Smith, was another notable

P.T. Barnum's Circus, the Greatest Show on Earth.

Connecticut personality. Son of a Guinea king, he was captured by enemies and sold into slavery. Brought to Connecticut, he obtained his freedom and, by careful saving, acquired a farm, three houses, and twenty sailing ships carrying river trade. He was one of the strongest men in our history; it was said that he easily carried a barrel of molasses on each shoulder.

Other notable Connecticut people are Emma Hart Willard, renowned educator, born in Berlin, Connecticut; Mrs. Hannah Smith, who drew up what has been called the first petition in this country against slavery; and her five learned and eccentric daughters—Hancy Zephina, Laurilla Aleroyla, Cyrinthia Sacretia, Julia Evelina, and Abby Hadassah. All achieved fame for their abolitionist and equal-suffrage work. Another, more famous abolitionist, fiery John Brown, was born near Cornwall.

Phelps Gateway, one of Yale's prized architectural treasures.

Teaching and Learning

In the heart of the city of New Haven is one of the notable educational institutions of the world. It had its small beginning in 1701 when several Connecticut clergymen, all graduates of Harvard University, gathered in Branford to discuss the founding of a college. Tradition says as each entered the room he placed some books on a table, saying, "I give these books for founding a college in this colony." At Killingworth (Clinton) in 1702, at the house of Abraham Pierson, the college officially began its work with one student.

When the Reverend Pierson died, the college was moved to Saybrook and called the Collegiate School. Here the first commencement was held. When the trustees of the college voted to move it to New Haven, the people of Saybrook tried to stop them forcibly. After the property was finally loaded on wagons, the people removed the planking from the bridges.

Nevertheless, the move to New Haven took place in 1716, and when Elihu Yale contributed a gift of merchandise worth 562 pounds, the institution was named in his honor. In 1887 it adopted the name Yale University.

Yale University was the first institution in America to award the Doctor of Philosophy degree (in 1862); it opened the first collegiate agricultural experiment station in America in 1847, and even earlier, in 1831, it opened its Gallery of Fine Arts, the first school and art gallery to be a part of an American college.

Among the distinguished alumni of Yale are William Howard Taft, John C. Calhoun, Samuel J. Tilden, Samuel F.B. Morse, Jonathan Edwards, Nathan Hale, Noah Webster, Eli Whitney, Stephen Vincent Benet, Thornton Wilder, and Sinclair Lewis.

Charles and Augustus Storrs provided land, buildings, and an endowment to start a college at Mansfield in 1881. It was first known as Storrs Agricultural College, later as Connecticut Agricultural College, Connecticut State College, and finally as the University of Connecticut at Storrs. With an impressive campus, it is one of the fastest growing educational institutions in the East.

One of the nation's four great armed services institutions is

The Coast Guard Academy is unique among military universities.

located in Connecticut. The Coast Guard Academy was established at New London in 1876. Part of the cadets' training is received on a sailing vessel—the picturesque old barque *Eagle*.

Today Connecticut has nearly fifty institutions of higher education and four state technical institutes. Among the more famous are Trinity College at Hartford, founded 1823; Wesleyan University, Middletown, founded in 1831; and Connecticut College, New London, dating from 1911.

Connecticut has pioneered in many important fields of education. The first theological seminary in America was founded at Bethlehem in 1738. The first law school in America was begun in 1782 at Litchfield. Graduates included dozens of high government officials, noted attorneys, and lawmakers. Miss Pierce's Academy at Litchfield, founded in 1792, was the first institution in America for the higher education of women. The first American school for the deaf was founded at West Hartford in 1817, and the first American camp for boys began at Washington in 1861.

The state's first public schools were established in New Haven in 1642 and at Hartford in 1643. Connecticut is distinguished for some of the finest private schools, such as Choate, Taft, and Hopkins Grammar School, at New Haven, which has developed from the third oldest school in the country.

Connecticut's distinguished educators include Dr. Eliphalet Nott, who served as president of Union College for sixty-three years; noted educator Henry Barnard, first United States commissioner of education; Prudence Crandall, persecuted for her pioneering work in teaching black girls but later given a four hundred dollar pension; the Reverend Joseph Bellamy, founder of the first theological seminary; and Tapping Reeve, who founded the first law school and was also one of the foremost American male champions of women's rights.

Sailing at Saybrook.

Enchantment of Connecticut

For those who visit Connecticut without much knowledge of what it is really like, there are many surprises. Most surprising is that this heavily populated and industrialized state should have such a large proportion of woodland, quiet areas, and almost untracked wilderness. The sunny, sandy beaches of Long Island Sound twist and curve for 245 miles (394 kilometers). No one in Connecticut is more than two hours driving time from a pleasant saltwater beach.

No motorist is more than a half hour's drive from a state park, and the state forests offer shady refuge from the many other sunnier summer enjoyments. There are also numerous opportunities for winter sports in the state.

Vigorous and energetic cities with many cultural advantages contrast with some of the finest small towns and villages in the world. Many of these have tongue-twisting Indian names or reflect the Old Testament, such as Goshen, Hebron, Bethany, Zoar, Canaan, or Lebanon. It is probable that nowhere in the United States are there more historic old homes in such a small area. Connecticut is proud of the more than one thousand homes that date back to Colonial days or earlier.

For these and many other reasons, vacation travelers eagerly spend nearly a billion dollars per year to enjoy themselves in the small state of Connecticut.

THE CAPITAL

Probably nowhere in America do the roots of freedom and democracy go deeper than in the region where Connecticut's first communities—Windsor, Wethersfield, and Hartford—came into being. The fine museums of the capital city have preserved much of the feeling of this history. In the magnificent building of the Connecticut State Library are portions of one of the country's most historic documents—the great, original Charter of Connecticut, once hidden in the Charter Oak. The visitor is transferred back to

Golf is a popular sport in Connecticut.

1636 by the first record of the General Court of Connecticut, preserved in the library. The library possesses a painting of George Washington by Gilbert Stuart and the table on which Abraham Lincoln signed the Emancipation Proclamation. This building also contains the Colt Collection of Firearms, one of the most complete of its kind anywhere.

Another outstanding historical library is that of the Connecticut Historical Society. One of the prized items in its collection is the sea chest on which the Mayflower Compact was signed.

The Wadsworth Athenaeum has been called by various authorities "one of the nation's leading art museums" and "the cultural center of the city." Its seventy galleries display fine collections of art from the sixteenth through the twentieth centuries, as well as collections

Architect Bulfinch's Old Capitol adds contrast to modern Hartford.

of earlier Egyptian and Oriental work. Its exhibits of ship models and early American furniture are also well known. The Watkinson Reference Library in the Wadsworth Atheneum has an invaluable collection which includes two hundred books printed before 1500.

Another unusual museum in the Hartford area is the Children's Museum at West Hartford. Here displays of natural science and historical items, especially of the Indians, are put together in a way to be particularly interesting to young people.

Although a number of trees have been recorded in history, few have had the fame of the Charter Oak—that great tree, 33 feet (10 meters) in circumference, which was blown down in 1856. A number of historic items were made from it. One of these is the ornate chair in the state capitol used by the lieutenant governor when he presides over the Senate. So many other items were claimed to have been made from the wood of this great tree that Mark Twain said he had seen "a walking stick, dog collar, needle-case, three legged stool, bootjack, dinner table, tenpin alley, toothpick, and enough Charter Oak to build a plank road from Hartford to Salt Lake City."

Where Charter Oak Avenue and Charter Oak Place meet in Hartford is located the Charter Oak Memorial, contributed by the Society of Colonial Dames: a large column of granite with the inscription "Near this spot stood the Charter Oak, known in the history of the Colony of Connecticut as the hiding place of the Charter, October 31, 1687."

Located in 41-acre (16.5-hectare) Bushnell Park is the golden-domed capitol building of Connecticut, built of marble and granite and completed in 1880. Its summit once was topped by the 15-foot (4.5-meter) statue *The Genius of Connecticut*. This was removed after the 1938 hurricane because officials feared it might crash through the roof of the building. A replica of this statue now stands in the north lobby.

Twelve marble statues are a unique and prominent feature of the outside of the capitol. These stand upon the angles of the dome at the base of the cone and represent agriculture, commerce, education, music, science, and force. Historic scenes are shown in bas-relief carvings on the outside, and there are also statues of many Connecticut leaders. The interior of the building is particularly noted for its exceptional floor designs.

A bronze statue of Nathan Hale, Connecticut's martyred school teacher, stands in the first floor corridor. Other items of interest are the Civil War battle flags in the Hall of Flags, the original headstone from the grave of General Israel Putnam, and the "portable bedstead" of General Lafayette.

One of the country's notable examples of fine architecture is the former capitol building, the Old State House, designed by New England architect Charles Bulfinch. The famous unsupported spiral staircase of this masterpiece was one of the marvels of its day.

St. Joseph's Cathedral in Hartford is the headquarters of the Roman Catholic Archdiocese of Connecticut.

Trinity College is a development of the first Episcopal college

The state capitol, built of granite and marble, was completed in 1879.

established in New England. The chapel of this college, completed in 1932, is one of the finest Gothic buildings in the country. While it was being built its builders held weekly meetings of all the workmen to remind them of the spiritual meaning of what they were doing. Prizes were given for the best wood sculpture by workmen on any subject the sculptor chose. These interesting pieces are now scattered about the building and its grounds.

Notable commercial buildings are numerous in the capital. Aetna Life Insurance Company built the world's largest structure of Colonial design for its headquarters. The Travelers Insurance Building was the tallest building in New England for many years. Phoenix Mutual Life Building is among the largest.

The house built by Mark Twain at a cost of $131,000 is open to the public as a memorial to Twain. Here he wrote *The Prince and the Pauper, Tom Sawyer, Huckleberry Finn,* and other books during his seventeen years residence. Twain built the servants' quarters and kitchen on the front of the house so the workers could "see the parade go by.... It saves time and wear on the rugs," was the author's explanation.

A porch of the house was built like a riverboat's pilothouse, a reminder of Twain's life on the Mississippi.

Colt Park is a memorial to the inventor of the revolver. The Colt memorial statue commemorates the first crude revolver model carved by Colt when he was a fifteen-year-old sailor.

Bushnell Memorial Hall was erected as a tribute to Dr. Horace Bushnell. It seats 3,227 people, and the interior is decorated with gold leaf and "barbaric design." The impressive Morgan memorial commemorates the long connection of the J.P. Morgan family with Hartford. One of the city's most unusual and touching memorials is the *Monument to a Mother,* a clock and chime tower built by Henry and Walter Kenny. It is said to be the first monument to a woman whose only claim to greatness was being a fine mother.

OTHER CENTRAL POINTS

Guilford has many old and interesting houses. The Old Stone House built by the Reverend Henry Whitfield about 1639 is believed to be the oldest stone house in the state and one of the oldest in the nation. It is now the Henry Whitfield State Historical Museum. Among the famous houses of Guilford are the many "salt box" houses that show the varying types of this typical New England structure. Other interesting houses are the "Sabbath Day" houses built in Guilford by outlying people who had to have a place to stay when they came to town for church. The Thomas Griswold House is another museum of early Americana, and the Farmers' Museum, displaying early farm equipment and a blacksmith shop, is just behind the house. Guilford's most famous politician was Samuel Hill, who ran for office so many times that the expression "running like Sam Hill" is said to have been coined about him.

One of the most scenic areas of the state is Ninevah Falls of the Hammonasset River near North Madison. Old Saybrook claims to be the fourth oldest town in Connecticut, and one of the principal places of historic interest there is Fenwick Point Lighthouse.

A fascinating historical sidelight concerns the boundary dispute between Old Lyme and New London. To save the expense of appealing to the courts to settle this boundary dispute, the towns agreed to let two men from each town have a fist fight. The champions from Lyme won the fight, and the boundary was moved to the Niantic River.

The old boundary had been at Bride's Brook. This took its name, according to tradition, from the incident when Governor Winthrop, who had no authority on the western bank, stood on his side of the brook and married a couple standing on the other side who could not cross over because the stream was flooded.

Pratt House at Essex dates from about 1725 and exhibits the fine Griswold collection of Early American furnishings.

William Gillette, son of Connecticut Senator Francis Gillette, was a great figure of the American stage and a Hartford native. At the peak of his career, in 1913, he began to build his "castle" near East Haddam. The granite walls are 5 feet (1.5 meters) thick at the base. Wooden locks on the doors appear to have been designed by Rube Goldberg. Everything about the house reflected the eccentric owner. Before his death Gillette said he hoped "that the property did not fall into the hands of some blithering saphead." He might be pleased to know that the property is now a state park.

East Haddam is the location of the famous Goodspeed Opera House, built in 1876 and still used for performances during the summer. Also at East Haddam is the little schoolhouse where Nathan Hale taught.

Durham still remembers the two church congregations that were rivals. Each attempted to build a church with a taller steeple. The south church managed to do this, but the story is told that a high wind picked up the steeple and tossed it point first through the roof of the church, in a kind of modern-day version of the Tower of Babel.

Insilco silver company, the largest manufacturer of sterling and silver plate in the world, is headquartered at Meriden. The city is said to have one of the most attractive natural settings of any city. Hubbard Park, east of Meriden, covers 900 acres (364 hectares) of the Hanging Hills, which reach heights of 1,000 feet (304.8 meters). In the park are Castle Craig, a stone observation tower, Merimere Reservoir, and a small zoo.

Among the distinctions of Middletown is its Olin Memorial Library, which possesses the only original manuscript of Einstein's theory of relativity. Kensington is known for the fact that it erected what was probably the nation's first monument to Civil War soldiers. It also boasted the first organ in New England.

New Britain is known familiarly as the Hardware City. It has a fine Children's Museum, with unusual ethnic exhibits called "Window on the World." Also at the museum is the Judd memorial collection of circus objects and models. New Britain has a fine Museum of American Art. Near the center of the city, in Walnut Hill Park, is the illuminated 97-foot (29.5-meter) high World War Memorial shaft, one of the finest monuments in the state. The park is also renowned for its rose gardens.

Farmington is especially well known for its houses of the 1600s and other fine period houses. The Farmington Museum and Hill-Stead Museum both exhibit objects connected with living in an earlier day. The Barney Memorial Library displays one of the country's most valuable collections of bird eggs. Included are the only dwarf screech owl eggs in the United States.

Bloomfield is noted for one of the most important and unique examples of modern commercial architecture. When it was finished in 1957, the Connecticut General Life Insurance Company building was ranked by the American Institute of Architects as one of "the ten buildings in America's future." Its unobstructed work spaces, green-tinted window walls, garden courts, and pools are fine examples of modern design. On a knoll of the landscaped grounds are red granite monoliths by the famous Japanese-American sculptor Isamu Noguchi.

Windsor, one of Connecticut's three original towns, exhibits the Fyler House and Wilson Museum. The house was built in 1640, one of the oldest houses in the state. One of the great religious organizations of the world had its beginning in Windsor. The First Congregational Church in Windsor was the first of that denomination anywhere.

A memorial in Enfield marks the location of the church where Jonathan Edwards preached his renowned sermon "Sinners in the Hands of an Angry God," which had much influence on the "Great Awakening" in the field of religion. Enfield was headquarters of the Society for the Detection of Horse Thieves and Robbers, founded in 1845. Its three hundred members agreed always to keep five hundred dollars in the treasury "for readiness in the pursuit of thieves when called upon." The bylaws state that a swift horse must always be kept ready for any emergency. The group was a great force for law and order in the region for many years.

NEW HAVEN

Any listing of the world's cultural centers must include New Haven, home of Yale University and its magnificent libraries and museums. In spite of its closeness to New York City, New Haven is a New England city, built around a typical New England Village green. The 16-acre (6.5-hectare) green is one of the outstanding features of the city, remaining just as it was platted by the original settlers. It is flanked on each of its four sides by Yale University and three distinctive churches. Center Congregational is considered a masterpiece of Georgian architecture.

One of Yale's outstanding attractions is the Peabody Museum, named often as "one of the world's greatest museums of natural history." One of its most valuable exhibits is the remains of a ground sloth, found with some of the hide and hair still clinging to it, which is most unusual. The great mural *The Age of Reptiles,* 110 feet (33.5 meters) long and 16 feet (4.9 meters) high, is the largest natural history mural ever created. Yale University Art Gallery is also one of the finest of its type.

The huge Yale Bowl is the scene of exciting Ivy League athletic events. It features the Walter Camp Memorial Gateway, honoring the "Father of American Football." Yale's Whitney Gym is said to be the largest building in the world devoted exclusively to athletics and physical training.

Sculpture by Isamu Noguchi on the Connecticut General Grounds.

Among attractions of the "Old Campus" at Yale is Connecticut Hall, where Nathan Hale (class of 1733) lived and studied. The landmark of the university is beautiful Harkness Tower, 221-foot (67.4-meter) memorial to Charles W. Harkness, class of 1883. It is called "the most distinguished structure of the University" by many critics.

Nearby in East Haven is the Branford Trolley Museum, where more than fifty old streetcars are displayed. Some are used to take visitors on trolley rides. Also at East Haven is the Old Mill Country

Store, an old-fashioned grocery store selling many items of a bygone time.

The city is flanked by West Rock and East Rock. The latter is 359 feet (109.4 meters) high and a mile and a half (2,414 meters) long. Here is East Rock Park, 647 acres (261.8 hectares) of natural beauty, providing excellent views of New Haven. Indian Head Peak was used by the Quinnipiac Indians for smoke signaling. The opposite area is now West Rock Nature Center, with woodland trails, ponds and meadows, and a fine zoo.

Reminders of New Haven's historic past are the many old cemeteries. Many of the famous people who once labored in the city are buried at Grove Street Cemetery, such as Noah Webster, Eli Whitney, Lyman Beecher, Samuel F.B. Morse, James D. Dana, and Charles Goodyear.

WESTERN CONNECTICUT

Bridgeport, settled in 1639, was named for the first drawbridge over the Pequonnock River. Today it has become the leading manufacturing city of a leading manufacturing state. Here are such mammoth manufacturers as Waranaco, Raybestos, Manhattan, Dictaphone, and Bridgeport Better Brass.

Memories of Bridgeport's most famous citizen—P.T. Barnum—are many. These include the Barnum Museum, where personal items of the showman, Tom Thumb, the old circus, and other phases of his promotional genius are displayed. Each year a Barnum Festival is held at Bridgeport in July, with concerts, parades, and art shows dedicated to the great Bridgeport booster. Tom Thumb is remembered by a statue—made to his exact size—mounted on a 10-foot (3-meter) shaft in Grove Cemetery, where both Tom and his wife are buried. Barnum is also buried in Grove Cemetery. This is the burial place of another Bridgeport resident, beloved composer Fanny Crosby, who was blind from her sixth year.

Bridgeport has a fine Museum of Art, Science and Industry, with a modern planetarium, placed in the sylvan setting of Ninety Acres

Park. Other parks are Seaside, with its seawall drive and Perry Memorial Arch, and wooded Beardsley Park, including a zoo.

Bridgeport was the scene of an interesting legend told of the life of George Washington. Arriving late and tired at the Pixlee Tavern, he found the dining room completely full—satisfied guests devouring the famous savory fried oysters. No one recognized the great general, who sat by the fireplace, growing more hungry every minute. Finally he remarked in a loud voice, "Do any of you gentlemen realize that horses are very fond of oysters?" There was a lively discussion on this point, and one guest offered a wager that "No horse ever lived that would eat oysters!"

"Very well," said Washington, "why not try them on my horse?" When the guests hurried out, Washington calmly took a place at the table and called for his oysters.

Stratford, named for Shakespeare's hometown in England, has gained world fame for its Shakespeare Festival Theater, where plays of the bard are given in a replica of an Elizabethan playhouse.

Norwalk is another industrial center, picturesquely situated on both sides of the island-fringed harbor at the mouth of the Norwalk River. Here is the house of Colonel Thomas Fitch, called the Yankee Doodle House because of Colonel Fitch's connection with that song. At Cedar Hammock Island, Nathan Hale set out on the daring mission from which he did not return. Nearby New Canaan is noted for the Silvermine Guild of Artists and the Silvermine Guild College of Art, one of the largest year-round cultural centers of the East. It offers exhibits and instruction in painting, sculpture, ceramics, design, and other related arts.

Large numbers of business and professional people commute from Stamford to New York City. Stamford is noted for its Museum and Nature Center, including a dairy farm, planetarium, zoo, observatory, art gallery, and nature trails.

Stamford's First Presbyterian Church is a magnificent structure of contemporary design. The exterior was inspired by the Christian symbol of a fish. Abstract colored glass windows extend from floor to vaulted ceiling, showing the crucifixion, the resurrection, and illustrations of Christ's teachings.

The First Presbyterian Church in Stamford.

Greenwich is a residential suburb just 28 miles (45 kilometers) from Times Square. It boasts many palatial landscaped estates. At Greenwich is the Putnam Cottage, from which General Putnam made his famous escape. Bruce Museum contains fine collections of the natural history of the state and of the Indians and Colonial times. Audubon Nature Center offers a nature preserve of 425 acres (172 hectares) with guided nature trail, museum, and bookstore. Putnam

Memorial State Park near Redding Ridge commemorates General Putnam's fiery speech that persuaded his men to remain at Connecticut's "Valley Forge."

Another early American museum is found at Danbury, especially famous for its doll house collection. Danbury has progressed greatly from the time the Indians were willing to sell the land where it stands for a bag of beans.

Near Sandy Hook is the only known Pootatuck Indian cemetery in Connecticut. Nearby residents had agreed to preserve this cemetery perpetually, but the Peabody Museum sent an archaeologist who soon was digging up the graves. The museum would not give up its excavation, until the community posted guards with shotguns at the cemetery and got a court order.

Waterbury, fourth largest city in Connecticut, is the home of Mattatuck Historical Museum with its collection of Whistler etchings and a junior museum with an apothecary shop.

Near Watertown lived spectacular James Bishop, who delighted in performing stunts that were once discussed in every New England home. He was noted for harvesting his 50-acre (20-hectare) hay field in one day, and people would swarm from miles around to help with the work and eat the five meals Mrs. Bishop served during the day. One year Bishop decided he would haul all of the hay in that pasture to New Haven in a single wagon load. He built a huge wagon, repaired bridges, cut down trees along the route, and moved a small building. Twelve yoke of oxen, wearing colored pennants, pulled the great wagon load, on which sat a band playing lively melodies. Bishop preceded the great hayrack in a coach heralded by outriders and cheered by hundreds of spectators, who told of the stunt for generations.

Wonderful views of the Housatonic Valley, southern Berkshires, Green Pond, and Candlewood Mountains are to be had from the top of Chicken Hill. This was named for Chief Chicken. If he lived today he would probably have to take many scalps to live down his name.

Litchfield has been named officially as one of America's "Historic Villages." It is said to be typical of an old New England town and one of the most beautiful in the nation. The Tapping Reeve House and

Law School was restored in tribute to the nation's first school for training members of the legal profession.

Kent Falls State Park in North Kent is considered to possess the most spectacular waterfall in the state. Cornwall was the site of the famous foreign mission school founded by Edwin W. Dwight. He was inspired to begin this school when he found the Hawaiian immigrant priest Henry Obookiah weeping on the steps of Yale University because a higher education was not open to him. Obookiah is buried at Cornwall.

Winsted is the mecca of flower lovers during its annual Laurel Festival, in tribute to the beautiful state flower.

EASTERN CONNECTICUT

East Thompson is known for its sports-car races. Putnam was named in honor of favorite son General Israel Putnam. Many Putnam memories abound in the region. Between Pomfret and Abington is the Wolf Den. Putnam and five of his neighbors were hunting a wolf which had caused much damage to chicken yards and sheep folds. The animal disappeared into this cave.

Putnam tied a rope around his waist and descended into the pit after the wolf. When fierce growls and shouts came from the depths of the cave, the neighbors dragged Putnam out by the rope, so hurriedly that they tore off his shirt and scratched his skin on the rocks. However, Putnam went back a second and then a third time. Finally a shotgun was heard reverberating within the confined walls, and Putnam was hauled to the surface grasping the wolf by its ears. The Daughters of the American Revolution have mounted a tablet on the Wolf Den entrance telling of the encounter.

At South Coventry the ten-room Nathan Hale Homestead is completely furnished as it might have been occupied by the Hale family. Many actual pieces of the Hale family pewter, china, silver, and furniture are preserved there.

Windham is known for the famous "battle of the frogs," the theme of many tales and ballads. The story is told that during the

Right: Nathan Hale Homestead in South Coventry. Below: The interior of the First Presbyterian Church in Stamford.

French and Indian wars the people of the town heard such a noise they thought Windham was being attacked and rushed out to defend their homes. They seemed to hear the repeated cry calling for the surrender of their two best-known attorneys: "Colonel Dyer and Elderkin, too," went the weird chant. After waiting all night for battle, their scouts found thousands of dead frogs in the dry basin of a nearby pond. For some unknown reason the frogs had fought a tremendous battle—probably to reach the remaining small puddle of water. This has been known as the Battle of the Frogs ever since.

Norwich was among the first cities given a charter in Connecticut. The city has always been a leader in industry. The first paper mill in the colony was opened there in 1766, and the first cut nails were produced there in 1772. Old Norwich town has been called a "museum of the past."

Leffingwell Inn at Norwich was owned by Thomas Leffingwell, one of Connecticut's most important Revolutionary War personages. Here many war councils were held. The inn has been restored and furnished with seventeenth and eighteenth century antiques. There is a museum in the basement.

Norwich is notable as the home of ancestors of five presidents of the United States: Fillmore, Grant, Hayes, Garfield, and Cleveland. According to legend, Norwich was the scene of an unusual event in 1823. The Thames River suddenly rose and washed away the Methodist chapel. It is reported to have sailed calmly down the river, with its lights still burning, past the astonished boat captains in Long Island Sound.

The cornerstone of the Norwich monument to loyal Chief Uncas was laid in 1833 by President Andrew Jackson. Another monument to an Indian chief is found near Norwich. Because of his friendship for the white man, Uncas was bitterly hated by Chief Miantonomo. By clever strategy Uncas captured Miantomono and turned him over to the colonial commissioners for trial. They condemned him to death and turned him back to Uncas, urging that "all mercy and moderation be exercised in the manner of his execution."

As Miantonomo walked back to the scene of his capture, he was killed with one blow of a hatchet and buried where he fell. For many years, each Indian who passed by placed a stone on a cairn in Mian-tonomo's memory. Now, near where he fell, is a stone monument erected to pay him tribute.

Chapman's Falls near North Plain is in one of the loveliest gorges in the state. Scenery of an entirely different kind is found not too far away at Rock Neck State Park—a fine saltwater beach. The Niantic River is noted particularly for its bay scallops.

New London is one of the nation's notable cities of the sea. What has been called "America's first naval battle" was fought off New London's shores. Today the Coast Guard Academy and the Whaling Museum keep alive the city's close ties with the ocean. Thames Science Center is a museum where the exhibits are "touchable."

In the broad reaches of the sunken Thames River, the crews of Yale and Harvard train for their famed race, and the race is held there each year. Also at New London is still to be seen the schoolhouse where Nathan Hale taught before going on his fatal mission. The Bolles family of New London preserved a tract of ancient trees and presented it to Connecticut College. This is now Connecticut Aboretum and Bolles Wood.

The Submarine Library and Museum at Groton includes models of famous submarines and displays that trace the history of submarines back to Alexander the Great. At the Groton Navy Atlantic Submarine Base, one of the outstanding features is the 135-foot (41-

Kent Falls

Mystic Seaport, a restored maritime village.

meter) high tank, filled with tons of saltwater, where men in training practice escaping from disabled subs. A 135-foot (41-meter) monument at Fort Griswold State Park near Groton pays tribute to the soldiers of the Revolution who lost their lives nearby.

Mystic Seaport has been called "The Williamsburg of the Sea." Here every care possible has been made to recreate an historic American town of the 1840s. The care and extent of this work has been comparable in many ways to that of the famous Williamsburg (Va.) restoration. This one, however, shows life in the old sailing and whaling days. Several aged sailing ships have come to rest in this perfect setting, and at the port the square-rigged *Joseph Conrad* serves as a classroom for sea explorers. Here are the last of the old-time whaling ships. Shipsmith's shop, sail loft, and chandlery all help to show what the sailing life was like in those days.

At Mystic Seaport, as in many other parts of Connecticut, most visitors feel a profound appreciation of the up-to-date state which thinks so kindly of its past that it makes possible fascinating excursions into our nation's heritage.

Handy Reference Section

Instant Facts

Became the 5th state, January 9, 1788
Capital—Hartford, founded 1633
Nickname—The Constitution State
State motto—*Qui transtulit sustinet* (He who transplanted still sustains)
State animal—Sperm whale
State bird—American robin
State tree—White oak
State flower—Mountain laurel
Area—5,009 square miles (12,973 square kilometers)
Rank in area—48th
State song—''Yankee Doodle Dandy''
Shoreline—618 miles (995 kilometers)
Greatest length (north to south)—75 miles (121 kilometers)
Greatest width (east to west)—90 miles (145 kilometers)
Geographic center—East Berlin, Hartford County
Highest point—2,380 feet (725 meters), south slope of Mount Frissell
Lowest point—Sea level
Number of counties—8
Population—3,551,000 (1980 projection)
Rank in population—24th
Population density—605 persons per square mile (234 persons per square
            kilometers), 1970 census
Rank in density—4th
Population center—Cheshire, New Haven County
Birthrate—12.2 per 1,000
Infant mortality rate—14.8 per 1,000 births
Physicians per 100,000—203

Principal cities—		
Bridgeport	160,311	(1975 estimate)
Hartford	148,576	(1975 estimate)
New Haven	137,707	(1970 census)
Stamford	108,798	
Waterbury	108,033	
New Britain	83,441	

You Have a Date with History

1614—Adriaen Block explores coastline, sails up Connecticut River
1631—Wahquinnacut urges European settlement in Connecticut Valley
1633—First forts and trading posts
1634—Wethersfield settled
1635—Beginnings of Hartford
1637—Pequot War
1638—New Haven founded
1639—Fundamental orders adopted
1662—Charter granted by Charles II
1675—King Philip's War
1687—Charter hidden in Charter Oak
1701—Beginnings of Yale University
1770—Lebanon freemen draft declaration of rights and liberties
1775—Revolutionary War begins; 31,939 from Connecticut serve
1781—Benedict Arnold heads British forces attacking Groton and New London
1784—Connecticut abolishes slavery
1786—Western lands ceded; Western Reserve property rights retained
1788—Became the fifth state
1795—First insurance company organized
1837—First railroad trains operated
1865—Civil War ends; 57,379 Connecticut men had served
1871—Samuel L. Clemens (Mark Twain) first occupies his home at Hartford
1881—Beginnings of University of Connecticut at Storrs
1901—Sumatra tobacco growing started
1910—Coast Guard Academy moved to New London
1917—World War I begins; 65,728 Connecticut men serve during war
1935—Tercentenary observed in statewide celebrations
1941—World War II begins; 210,891 Connecticut men and women serve
1954—First atomic submarine launched at Groton
1960—County governments abolished
1965—Third Constitutional Convention held (others in 1818 and 1902)
1968—Atomic energy plant opens at Haddam Neck
1975—Ella T. Grasso takes office as governor (first woman governor without family ties to the office)

The American Shakespeare Theater in Stratford.

Thinkers, Doers, Fighters

People of renown who have been associated with Connecticut

Allen, Ethan
Barnum, Phineas Taylor
Bartlett, Paul Wayland
Beecher, Henry Ward
Burritt, Elihu
Cleaveland, Moses
Clemens, Samuel (Mark Twain)
Colt, Samuel
Crosby, Fanny
De Koven, Reginald
Fitch, John
Gillette, Francis
Gillette, William
Goodyear, Charles
Greene, Jacob L.
Hale, Nathan
Hepburn, Katharine
Hitchcock, Lambert H.
Howe, Elias
Huntington, Collis P.
Ingersoll, Simon

Lyon, Nathaniel
MacDonough, Thomas
Morgan, J. Pierpont
Palmer, Nathaniel B.
Pratt, Francis A.
Putnam, Israel
Reeve, Tapping
Seabury, Samuel
Sherman, Roger
Stowe, Harriet Beecher
Terry, Eli
Thomas, Seth
Trumbull, Jonathan
Uncas (Chief)
Walcott, Oliver
Waramaug (Chief)
Webster, Noah
Willard, Emma Hart
Winthrop, John, Jr.
Yale, Linus

Governors of the State of Connecticut

Samuel Huntington 1786-1796
Oliver Wolcott 1796-1797
Jonathan Trumbull II 1797-1809
John Treadwell 1809-1811
Roger Griswold 1811-1812
John Cotton Smith 1812-1817
Oliver Wolcott, Jr. 1817-1827
Gideon Tomlinson 1827-1831
John S. Peters 1831-1833
Henry W. Edwards 1833-1834
Samuel A. Foot 1834-1835
Henry W. Edwards 1835-1838
Wm. W. Ellsworth 1838-1842
Chauncey F. Cleveland 1842-1844
Roger S. Baldwin 1844-1846
Isaac Toucey 1846-1847
Clark Bissell 1847-1849
Joseph Trumbull 1849-1850
Thomas H. Seymour 1850-1853
Charles H. Pond 1853-1854
Henry Dutton 1854-1855
William T. Minor 1855-1857
Alexander H. Holley 1857-1858
Wm. A. Buckingham 1858-1866
Joseph R. Hawley 1866-1867
James E. English 1867-1869
Marshall Jewell 1869-1870
James E. English 1870-1871
Marshall Jewell 1871-1873
Charles R. Ingersoll 1873-1877
Richard D. Hubbard 1877-1879
Charles B. Andrews 1879-1881
Hobart B. Bigelow 1881-1883

Thomas M. Waller 1883-1885
Henry B. Harrison 1885-1887
Phineas C. Lounsbury 1887-1889
Morgan G. Bulkeley 1889-1893
Luzon B. Morris 1893-1895
O. Vincent Coffin 1895-1897
Lorrin A. Cooke 1897-1899
George E. Lounsbury 1899-1901
George P. McLean 1901-1903
Abiram Chamberlain 1903-1905
Henry Roberts 1905-1907
Rollin S. Woodruff 1907-1909
George L. Lilley 1909
Frank B. Weeks 1909-1911
Simeon E. Baldwin 1911-1915
Marcus H. Holcomb 1915-1921
Everett J. Lake 1921-1923
Chas. A. Templeton 1923-1925
Hiram Bingham 1925
John H. Trumbull 1925-1931
Wilbur L. Cross 1931-1939
Raymond E. Baldwin 1939-1941
Robert A. Hurley 1941-1943
Raymond E. Baldwin 1943-1946
Wilbert Snow 1946-1947
James L. McConaughy 1947-1948
James C. Shannon 1948-1949
Chester Bowles 1949-1951
John Lodge 1951-1955
Abraham Ribicoff 1955-1961
John Dempsey 1961-1971
Thomas J. Meskill 1971-1975
Ella T. Grasso 1975-

Index

94

PICTURE CREDITS

ABOUT THE AUTHOR

With the publication of his first book for school use when he was twenty, **Allan Carpenter** began a career as an author that has spanned more than 135 books. After teaching in the public schools of Des Moines, Mr. Carpenter began his career as an educational publisher at the age of twenty-one when he founded the magazine *Teachers Digest.* In the field of educational periodicals, he was responsible for many innovations. During his many years in publishing, he has perfected a highly organized approach to handling large volumes of factual material: after extensive traveling and having collected all possible materials, he systematically reviews and organizes everything. From his apartment high in Chicago's John Hancock Building, Allan recalls, "My collection and assimilation of materials on the states and countries began before the publication of my first book." Allan is the founder of Carpenter Publishing House and of Infordata International, Inc., publishers of *Issues in Education* and *Index to U. S. Government Periodicals.* When he is not writing or traveling, his principal avocation is music. He has been the principal bassist of many symphonies, and he managed the country's leading non-professional symphony for twenty-five years.